Climbing

THE DEFINITIVE GUIDE TO DROPPING NAMES, PUTTING ON AIRS, SCALING THE SOCIAL LADDER, AND ESCAPING THE DRAB, VULGAR EXISTENCE OF EVERYDAY MIDDLE-CLASS LIFE

MICHAEL RYAN

Illustrations by George Moran

ADDISON-WESLEY PUBLISHING COMPANY

Reading, Massachusetts   Menlo Park, California   London
Amsterdam   Don Mills, Ontario   Sydney

Portions of this material originally appeared in slightly different form in *Boston Magazine.*

Library of Congress Cataloging in Publication Data
Ryan, Michael, 1950—
  Climbing, the definitive guide to dropping names, putting on airs, scaling the social ladder, and escaping the drab, vulgar existence of respectable middle-class life.
    1. Success—Anecdotes, facetiae, satire, etc.
I. Title.
PN6231.S83R9   818 .5402   80-19183
ISBN 0-201-06136-8 (pbk.)

Designed by Betty Binns Graphics.

ISBN 0-201-06136-8   ABCDEFGHIJ-WZ-89876543210

TO D.G.R.
FOR KEEPS

Acknowledgments

When J. Whitney Stillman announced, at an Upper East Side party a decade ago, that he was looking at the greatest collection of Pretentati he had ever seen, he certainly had no idea that he was inventing a book as well as a word. Nonetheless, he should be held morally, if not legally, liable for planting the seed that grew into this book; my lawyers will doubtless attempt to use that as a defense.

My wife, Debora, who has grown used to being awakened by the noise of a typewriter steaming away in the middle of the night, read most of this book and had the tact not to give me her frank and valued criticism of the manuscript, for which I shall be eternally grateful.

Last, but not least, I must pin the blame on my editor, Dorothy L. Coover, AKA Doe. It was her idea. It really was. I didn't want to do it. She made me. I'll tell everything. She did it. Just don't send me to the chair. She did it. Really. . .

Contents

Preface

Democracy is to social climbing as manure is to a rosebush. A society in which everybody theoretically is equal to everybody else is a society in which everyone will fight like hell to be more equal than the guy next door—and to be sure everybody knows it.

Jefferson and his ilk had no idea what they were letting us in for, else they might not have been so nasty to George III. After all, in a well-ordered tyranny, every serf knows his place and sticks to it; society is blissfully simple. If you are born a bilge monkey, you know you will always remain a bilge monkey and damned lucky to get the job. If you are born King of Kings, Light of the Aryans, Shadow of the Almighty, and Heir to the Peacock Throne, you know that generations yet unborn will call you blessed. At least it works that way in theory. The system is simple, elegant, and easy to understand.

In a democracy, on the other hand, any jackass can grow up to achieve the Blessed Trinity of Fame, Money, and Power—even if he was born in the house his father built and went to Whittier College. Distinctions of class, rank, and social standing were so repugnant to the framers of the Constitution that they specifically forbade the federal government to create them. For the two hundred years since then, Americans have been striving desperately to remedy that error.

We are a nation of snobs. Take John Smith, in his

white frame house in Anytown, U.S.A., with its white picket fence out on Main Street. Scratch him deep, and you'll find a closet aristo who mourns in his heart of hearts that he wasn't born Lord Smith of Anytown. Why, he wonders, couldn't he trade his gray felt fedora for a coronet, his picket fence for a palace gate, and even his faithful Lassie for a well-trained brace of blood-hounds? He sees himself in his daydreams at El Morocco, Annabel's, and Skorpios. In his modest fantasies he imagines how pleasant it would be if the townsfolk— old Mr. Whipple, kindly Uncle John, Mrs. Brown, and Cousin Sarah—would just touch their foreheads defer-entially to the ground whenever he passes.

There are closet snobs like John Smith in every town and hamlet in America—and you are probably one of them. You fancy yourself a jet-setter because you buy your socks from England instead of at Woolworth's. You count yourself a sophisticate because you say *tom-aahhhto* and read the *Christian Science Monitor*, and an epicure because none of your wine bottles has a twist-off cap. Your *1812 Overture* record makes you an aesthete. Sad news, my friend: that kind of action will never get you into Xenon, land your face on the cover of *W*, or get you invited to Antibes for the weekend. If you, like most of us, were not to the manor born—if your mother dyes her hair brown instead of blue—you need plenty of help. Frankly, unless you get lucky and win the Principality of Monaco from Philippe Junot in a game of snooker, you're headed straight for nowhere.

It doesn't have to be that way. Out there are millions just like you, eager to climb to their own rightful place in society (so many, in fact, that they have formed their own colony, Manhattan). Until now, writers have ignored you. They have told you how to pick running shoes and how to get the cellulite out of your fanny, but they've never told you what you really want to know: how to leave your ordinary, decent, middle-class lives behind and climb to the vulgar superficiality of life among the glitzy, the rich, the in.

These are the people whose society you covet: Creatures of fawnlike grace and faunlike seductiveness. Stars whose autographs Mick Jagger covets and whose company Garbo seeks. Men who can monarchize, be feared, and kill with looks; women whose faces launch a thousand ships — and people of both genders who already *own* a thousand ships and race them for the America's Cup. This is your dream, your goal, your life — to be as one of them. A marvelous dream, indeed.

Impossible, you say? Not any longer. Rejoice, your time has come. This book will be your guide on the long climb upward. The journey will be trying, difficult, and treacherous, but you can do it. Remember, even Jay Gatsby was once the humble midwestern kid Jimmy Gatz. If you follow the lessons in this handbook carefully, you can end up just the way he did.

Preparing for the ascent

A field guide to the Beautiful People

The first step in every successful social climb is deciding where you're headed. Remember, there is no single elite in American society, but three or four or more. Your first task is to decide which group you want to make it with and aim accordingly.

If your great desire in life has always been to hob-nob with John Travolta, learning how to deal with Mrs. Vanderbottom's butler will be a useless exercise. If you aspire to be the talk of Race Week at Newport, getting your sequined jumpsuit from Liza's couturier will hardly enhance your ambitions. Know the group you want to crack and stick with it.

In descending order of interest to the determined climber, these groups are:

THE GLITTERATI   These are the people who made Studio 54 a household word; if they can enjoy an unsavory old shed in a sleazy part of New York run by two guys from hunger, they can certainly learn to love you. These are the people who are on a first-name basis with Halston, although they never wear his clothes. They can tell you the location of every Fiorucci on the face of the globe. They use liberal amounts of controlled substances, and the drugs have inexplicable effects on their brains—

many of them think that Margaret Trudeau is interesting. They put wheels on their shoes and skate into traffic. They pay twenty dollars for an eighty-nine-cent Fruit of the Loom T-shirt with Judy Garland's picture on it. They bake amyl nitrate into brownies for Steve Rubell and often read *Women's Wear Daily*. Their Classic Example: Bianca Jagger.

THE PRETENTATI   These are the people who imagine themselves to be creatures of extreme wit, sophistication, and charm. Most of them read the *New York Review of Books*; the more unfortunate write it. Their favorite slapstick comedian is Dick Cavett, and they quote frequently from Baudelaire. During the Vietnam era, they signed petitions opposing the war that appeared each Sunday in the *New York Times*, to be

consumed by their friends with *brioches* and *café filtre*. Nowadays, some worry about nuclear power, others campaign to save the blue-eyed truffle boar. They are unstintingly *engagé*, taking forthright stands on the major issues of the day, such as *Truman v. Gore*, *Hellman v. McCarthy*, and *Podhoretz v. Epstein*. Each member of the group thinks he's Norman Mailer. Their Classic Example: Norman Mailer.

NATURE'S NOBILITY

The major flaw in our democracy is that we lack a hereditary peerage; this forces us to choose our own leaders. Luckily, the existence of *Nature's Nobility* means that the choice rarely requires real effort. Occasionally a candidate comes along whose clear combination of intelligence, humanity, talent, perception, and basic  decency makes him or her an obvious choice for an office of high public trust (the last such person was Abraham Lincoln.) But *Nature's Nobility* offers the next best thing to true excellence: superior dental work, good advertising, and charisma (whatever that may be). *Nature's Nobility* are those people who, before the big election—or the big promotion or the big contract, since politics isn't their only game—present themselves as creatures of charm, self-possession, and unquestionable presence. After the election—or promotion, or whatever—they lead us into disasters. But they do it with such grace that nobody notices. Their Classic Example: John Lindsay.

OLD MONEY   Every city has them. These are the people whose names sound like brokerage houses and whose grandfathers made it possible for everybody else's grandparents to come to this country—in steerage, to carry their hods. These are the people who drink martinis, join clubs, and are written about by John Cheever (although they are largely incapable of reading him). They are unfailingly polite, unerringly boring, and will mention, by way of making you feel at ease, that they once had a stableboy with the same last name as yours. Their Classic Example: anyone whose first name sounds like a last name.

THE MERITOCRATS

These are the people who make it on native ability, hard work, and fair play. They rise to high positions in public and private enterprise and are much esteemed for their integrity. They run foundations and  hospitals, chair committees, and make society move; and they work at it ceaselessly. This kind of devotion to duty is the last thing a true climber needs. Avoid it. Their Classic Example: Alger Hiss.

If you aspire to join this last group, please close this book, enroll in Harvard Law School, make *Law Review*, clerk for a Supreme Court justice, avoid the company of Bob Woodward, and wait for good things to happen. If you have what it takes to be Naturally Noble, run for mayor of New York and stop bothering me. But if you want to be a *Glitterato* or *Pretentato*, or if you want to find the side-door entrance to *Old Money* (it's hard to do much more than marry into it without taking the issue up with your forebears), read on. This book is for you. Only you can decide which category to aim for, of course. If, like most well-prepared climbers, you left your conscience in your mother's attic with your high school yearbook, you should have no ethical problem in choosing one of these courses.

If you are considering cracking the *Glitterati*, accept my compliments. You have probably chosen wisely. Most successful climbers choose this group; the admissions requirements are lax—and frequently waived altogether, a fact that will come in handy since you, like most climbers, probably have little in the way of accomplishments to recommend you.

To make it with the *Glitterati*, you need a gimmick. Not a *talent*, mind you, but a gimmick. For example, you might present yourself as a street-smart, leather-clad, unwashed hustler with a Brooklyn accent and an incoherent rage against the police that can be interpreted by credulous *Glitterati* as an incipient Marxist consciousness. If you adopt this style and flaunt it at just a few well-chosen *boîtes*, you will be discovered by Andy Warhol in short order and cast in his next film as a street-smart Brooklyn tough who falls in love with the Empire State Building. Nobody will ever see the film, of course, but the *Glitterati* will all recognize your face from the cover of *Interview*. Lee Radziwill will invite you to her next wedding, and William Sloane Coffin will praise the purity of your social conscience.

Still, if a Brooklyn accent doesn't come trippingly to your tongue, despair not. There are many other tricks in the *Glitterati* book. Suing or being sued by Gore Vidal is a popular gimmick; so is selling cocaine at a discount. You can certainly develop a *shtick* of your own with a little patience. As long as you have one, the *Glitterati* won't care who you are or where you came from—they assume you came from nowhere, just like they did.

The *Pretentati*, on the other hand, are a tougher case. In theory, of course, the *Pretentati* have reached their station in life because of some special talent, some signal accomplishment. Norman Mailer wrote a novel once; Salvador Dali used to dabble in art, and everybody thinks that George Plimpton must do something.

This admissions requirement will present you with only a momentary discomfiture. To circumvent it, merely remember always to pretend to a talent other than the one professed by the person you are dealing with. At the opening of Warhol's Whitney Museum retrospective, palm yourself off as a writer. Tell Nureyev you're a painter as you worm your way into his table at Elaine's. If you run into Cyrus Vance in a Southampton disco, tell him you're a composer. Hint to Susan Sontag that you're a diplomat. And so forth.

Don't worry that anybody will check out your claims. Pretensions to artistic or intellectual achievement are all the *Pretentati* demand—not achievement itself.

Occasionally, the *Pretentati do*; they are never *judged* on what they do, but they *do*. Tony Armstrong-Jones clicks away with his Brownie, and everybody thinks that's fine; find yourself a pretension, and everyone will think you're fine, too. Deep down, the *Pretentati* are nothing but *Glitterati* with delusions of competence.

The *Old Money*, of course, either do or do not do—it makes little difference, really; they can afford either. Except in New York, though, where decadence is a popular trait among the Old Money and a squandered life guarantees that some *New Yorker* writer will come along and romanticize you in a postmortem biography, you must at least *pretend* to do. That should come easily to you—after all, pretense is your vocation.

Testing your fitness

So now you know where you're headed—but believe me, you're not there yet. Knowing the name of the maître d' at La Côte Basque may get you the hors d'oeuvres, but you will need more than that to gain your social entrée. In the following pages we will discuss what it really takes: the airs and affectations (call them manners, please) you will have to learn, the uniforms you must wear and connections you must cultivate, the past you must fabricate, and the education you must fake to make your ascent a simple matter.

To begin, though, we must ensure that you are indeed fit to make the climb. The air gets awfully thin up there, and only the strong survive in the competition of world-class climbers. As a climber, you will be striv-

ing for the grand slam of American accomplishment: Fame, Money, and Power. Any one of them is attainable to those who will not stint, but you will feel more comfortable with all three. After all, any camel jockey in Araby is rich; even Richard Nixon had power, and as for fame, what have you heard from Deanna Durbin lately?

But *basta*. Not everybody can aspire to the Big Three—and if you can't, you'd better find out now, before you've blown the rent money having Dr. Howard Bellin rearrange your face so that it no longer resembles a textbook example of cubism. What's the use of climbing if you'll never be more than just a pretty face?

The following quizzes are designed to test your climbing aptitude. If you find yourself responding positively to the vast majority of the questions, clearly climbing is for you! If you don't, well, then, there's nothing disreputable about staying back home in Boise.

FAME

Fame. For generations Americans have distrusted it healthily. "How foolish to be somebody," Emily Dickinson sighed. "How public, like a frog." Well, my friend, practice your croaking. If you are going to be a successful climber, you will have to go public in a big, big way.

Use the following questions to see whether you can handle adulation:

1. I feel lost without my entourage. T___ F___

2. I've got to run, my motorcade is waiting. T___ F___

3. Nothing lulls me to sleep better than a cheering crowd beneath my window. T___ F___

4. Ron Galella is cute. T___ F___

5. I've got to do something about the radiator in the throne room. T___ F___

6. My *People* cover looked better this time. T___ F___

7. Henry Fonda/Lauren Bacall is playing me in the one-man/-woman show. ·T___ F___

8. I wear industrial-strength Foster Grants. T___ F___

9. I don't *care* if Garbo and the Beatles are doing it; I just don't do gigs anymore. T___ F___

10. I've found a new shampoo that's *great* for ticker tape. T___ F___

11. I'm tired of people ripping off my logo. T___ F___

12. I'm tired of people ripping off my clothes. T___ F___

13. If I can't be there to throw out the first ball, the President will be glad to fill in. T___ F___

14. I'll sue Grauman's if that damn cement doesn't wash off. T___ F___

15. I'm gonna hit one over the fence for that little kid at Children's Hospital. T___ F___

16. My wife/husband had better renounce her/his title by Friday, or else. T___ F___

17. The *National Enquirer* says I have four months to live. T___ F___

18. The family hasn't been the same since Uncle Edward abdicated. T___ F___

19. The family hasn't been the same since Uncle Carmine was rubbed out. T___ F___

20. The Pope calls me to cure his scrofula. T___ F___

Score yourself as follows: 0–5 True—become an *éminence grise*; 6–10 True—you'll be on the Merv Griffin Show any day; 11–15 True—you're probably Johnny's guest host; 16 and above True—your autograph is worth more than most people's houses.

MONEY

Fame often brings with it enough money to allow you to live comfortably. But for some climbers enough is not enough. You may be the sort of climber who needs money in abundant supply, the way an orchid needs water or a buzzard needs carrion. Diagnose yourself with this simple test:

1. I always smash the crystal goblets in the fireplace after a toast.   T____ F____

2. I always smash the breakfast china in the fireplace after the toast.   T____ F____

3. I've painted a day of the week on each of my houses.   T____ F____

4. My favorite snack is *Fritos avec de foie gras*.   T____ F____

5. They subdivided Daddy's summer place and called it Palm Springs.   T____ F____

6. My social secretary doesn't understand me.   T____ F____

7. Pearl Buck wanted me to adopt a foster country.   T____ F____

8. The President asked whether he could put the national debt on my Carte Blanche.   T____ F____

9. My petty cash account is a member, FDIC.   T____ F____

10. My servants have formed a union.   T____ F____

11. For Christmas I'm having my chaplain made a bishop.   T____ F____

12. I bought Nelson Bunker Hunt's old silver.   T____ F____

13. We need new peacocks for the lawn.   T____ F____

14. When it's noon at the gatehouse, it's three o'clock in my living room.　　T___ F___

15. My Uncle Tom's cabin was named Monticello.　　T___ F___

16. We're having the New York Philharmonic over to play for our anniversary party.　　T___ F___

17. They're staying in the guest house.　　T___ F___

18. I'm having my car overhauled; it doesn't fit Amtrak's new rails.　　T___ F___

19. We have to repaint the downstairs squash court.　　T___ F___

20. John Kenneth Galbraith does my household budget.　　T___ F___

Score yourself as follows: 1–5 True—settle for a split-level in Scarsdale; 6–10 True—why not relax with a six-pack of Mercedes?; 11–15 True—your butler has just hired a butler; 16 and above True—you can get a free Morgan Bank with the purchase of an electric toaster.

POWER

Not everybody needs power, and not everybody wants it. It got Marie Antoinette nowhere, lost Charles I his head, and left Mussolini hanging, after all. But power has its benefits; it left King Farouk the world's richest refugee, made King Constantine the toast of Mayfair, and even made Richard Nixon's crimes pardonable.

Test your potential for power with the following simple quiz:

1. I do solemnly swear to preserve, protect, and defend the Constitution of the United States from all enemies, foreign and domestic.　　　　　T___　F___

2. Whatsoever I shall loose on earth will be loosed in heaven, and whatsoever I shall bind on earth shall be bound in heaven.　　　　　T___　F___

3. I'm ordering an Olympic boycott.　　　T___　F___

4. Send Luca Brazzi to sleep with the fishes.　T___　F___

5. I'll send in the Marines to get that lawn mower back from next door.　　　　T___　F___

6. Rosebud.　　　　　　　　　T___　F___

7. Cancel "Charlie's Angels."　　　　T___　F___

8. I'm going to call Werner Erhard on the carpet and chew him out.　　　　　T___　F___

9. I have a nine-piece modular casting couch.　T___　F___

10. The last time we played "Family Feud", I had my consort beheaded.　　　　T___　F___

11. Tell the Joint Chiefs of Staff to serve the drinks until the waiters show up.　　　T___　F___

12. I'm playing golf with Billy Graham on Friday. T___ F___

13. The Gang of Four is my bridge club. T___ F___

14. Tell the Poet Laureate I need a new anthem. T___ F___

15. Buy Chile. T___ F___

16. I wore out the rubber stamp I use for excommunication decrees. T___ F___

17. For my Fourth of July party, I'm setting off some MX missiles in the backyard. T___ F___

18. The kids are having a slumber party in the Lincoln Room. T___ F___

19. I'm giving myself another Order of Lenin for the Mayday Parade. T___ F___

20. Tell the warden to get my color TV fixed right now—or else. T___ F___

Score yourself as follows: 1–5 True—try for a place on the county water board; 6–10 True—you are cut out to be an assistant producer, assistant secretary of state, or *consigliere*; 11–15 True—try for Speaker of the House; 16 and above True—President of the United States, *capo di tutti capi*, or chairman of Columbia Pictures.

Your climbing gear

The climber's uniform

Look about you. Consider the world you are eager to leave. Men with bellies like medicine balls in misshapen knit shirts with crocodiles nibbling at their nipples wander around swilling light beer and flipping Muriel Corona ashes on their running shoes. The shoes, of course, are Adidas, with their brand name emblazoned in plastic on the heel and their identity assured by bright stripes along the side. Women whose sunglasses trumpet the insignia of one French sweetboy and whose shifts advertise another stand around grinding out pastel cigarettes with the toes of their Anne Klein espadrilles.

This is the great American middle class, raised on advertising and transformed by circumstance into a series of walking human commercials. The names of their automobiles are printed in foot-high letters along the side and underscored by racing stripes, lest any passerby miss the point that the car is a *Le Car*. Their coffee comes from anthroponymic machines that Joe

DiMaggio has told them about. They even litter their homes and poolsides with copies of the *oeuvres* of Judith Krantz in decorator colors to match any interior scheme.

We were all indoctrinated—at least, those of us who had television instead of a governess for a baby-sitter—to believe in buying brand names; in the last decade or so we have begun to believe in *wearing* them. There is a vast land out there, stretching for thousands of miles, farther than the eye alone can see, whose inhabitants believe that Gloria Vanderbilt's name on their behinds will assure them of social status. This land is called Suburbia, and your job is to get out of it—fast. You can start by learning how to dress.

There is an old British Army story, set—as are all British Army stories—in Shepheard's Hotel in Cairo. A major is discovered running down the corridor stark naked, in pursuit of a similarly denuded young lady. Promptly hauled up on charges, the officer looks like a sure candidate for the brig, until he presents his defense: a passage from the Rules and Regulations that ordains that "an officer shall always be attired in the uniform appropriate to the activity in which he is engaged."

You will find this a useful ordinance to obey—or at least a good excuse when you are caught with your pants down. But it has a serious import, as climbers throughout history have discovered. Remember the biblical Joseph, whose coat of many colors (purchased, no doubt, at Sulka's of Babylon) made him the toast of Mesopotamia, snagging him dates with starlets and assuring him access to the best coke around. That coat, you recall, almost led to his downfall, when Joseph's brothers—heavy into the punk look—dumped him into the local well. As Joseph discovered, it doesn't pay to wear *Glitterati* clothes to a *Pretentati* party.

It is impossible to tell you exactly what clothes to wear on your climbing expedition, unless, of course, you are aiming at that staid section of *Old Money* or *Pretentati* types who lease their bodies for life to Ann Taylor or Brooks Brothers and never bother about clothing again. For this set, though, a few basic no-nos must be observed.

The only names that should appear on a piece of clothing are yours and your tailor's. Thus: "Made expressly for John D. Climber by Fustian & Snobbish, Clothiers." If, in fact, your clothes are not really bespoke, at least have the labels printed up and sew them in yourself.

The corollary of this rule, of course, is that all clothing labels should be *inside* the clothing. In your case, this is a positive advantage, since it allows you to pass off your frock from the irregulars section of Herbie's Bargain Bazaar as a Givenchy. If by some accident or other you do have a respectable label, you can make a show of removing the garment with the label prominently displayed. But for God's sake take care which garment you remove and where.

Another rule to remember is camouflage: wear the colors of the season and the terrain. For more formal occasions, this will simply mean sticking to dark, conservative colors. For summertime, especially in the great East Coast game preserves of the *Pretentati* and *Old Money* such as Martha's Vineyard and Everyhampton, choose your color scheme from your grocer's citrus counter: lime greens, lemon yellows, throbbing oranges are the shades you need, accented, if you are a woman, with a citrusy yarn in your hair.

Old Money parties are blessedly simple: everybody wears what his or her grandparent wore to the same party fifty years ago. The story is told of the dowager whose daughter-in-law (read climber-in-law) presented her with a new hat at Christmas. "But, my dear, I already have a hat," she declared, confused. Among the *Old Money*, if you don't already have a hat, buy one from somebody's estate.

Finally, if you don't know how to dress for the evening, take lessons from the waiters at your local Plaza or Ritz Hotel and from the lady who plays the cocktail piano. For women, a decent evening gown will cover most occasions, but too many male climbers have floundered by not knowing the difference between black tie and white tie and when to wear which. Suffice it to say that if you show up at a black-tie bash in white tie, or vice versa, you will be mistaken for the head-waiter. Remember also never to call your dinner jacket a tuxedo, and for God's sake turn down any invitation that specifies dress as semiformal—it probably means bowling shirt and cummerbund.

Unlike the *Pretentati* and *Old Money*, the *Glitterati* play in a faster league, where change is constant and failure to observe it is social death. Just a few years ago, if you arrived at a *Glitterati* party with a safety pin through your nose, Jann Wenner would have put you on the cover of *Rolling Stone* and hailed you as the musical genius of the age—whether or not you could play a note. Today, of course, you would be hustled off to the psycho ward—and nobody would remember who Jann Wenner was anyway.

Putting on your first—rarefied—airs

Once properly attired, you must face the vexing problem of presenting the proper visage to the society you're trying to crack. It could be curtains if in the middle of your very first debutante party (a fête so encrusted with strict rituals and rules that all fainthearted climbers should avoid one until graduating from this course) you let it slip that your mother plays bingo instead of bridge.

What you need is style, a package of the proper airs. Roots. Mannerisms. Accents. Words. Tastes and affectations that take the place of character among the upwardly mobile.

Your first temptation as you set out on the long climb upward will be to affect the mannerisms of the upper classes. Sound thinking—*if* you understand the mannerisms of the upper classes. If you are like most Americans, however, you will fall flat on your face immediately. Your mistake: adopting the fruity trill and flouncing gait that the unwashed often think typifies people of the better sort—a set of gaudy and outrageous movements and voice-box emanations copped from Margaret Dumont and the broad-beamed dowagers of movieland.

Dear friend, the perpendicular-pinkie-at-teatime may cut the caviar on the silver screen—Hollywood and polite society haven't even a nodding acquaintance—but don't expect it to get you anywhere in the real world, or even in the unreal world you're trying to enter. The dowager trill is as dated as the whalebone corset; and nowadays, if you talk like Julia Child, you'd better cook like she does, too.

Evaluate your position, referring to the previous diagnostic quizzes, and decide on the proper style of climb for you. There is an almost unlimited number of styles to choose from. You'll find they differ mainly in plumage, not principle. Here are just a few:

The George Bush. Perhaps the ultimate triumph of style over substance, the *Bush* is especially favored among those trying to crack the *Pretentati* by posing as concerned members of the eastern power elite with little real talent but ineffable wellsprings of goodwill. (Remember, by the way, that pretensions to wealth go over big with the *Pretentati*.)

The *Bush*, when combined with a gray business suit (on either a man or a woman), works wonders at museum openings, political bashes, or film screenings (see Part the Third for instructions on Gate-crashing). If you can master the preppy twang it demands—scrunching your *a*'s like the folds of an accordion and delivering the ends of sentences with the space between the top of your mouth and your cheeks wrinkled up so as to nasalize your syllables—you are in clover. When you utter horrible malapropisms at art openings—confusing Manet with Monet, for instance, or thinking Jasper Johns is a pigment—people will indulgently assume that your sheltered background is to blame. When you let loose with a stream of asininities at a political rally, Republicans will assume you are one of their own and nominate you for vice-president. Since Americans are genetically incapable of crediting high-born WASPs with the intelligence to be devious, they will always give you the benefit of the doubt and welcome you as an ornament to every social occasion.

Perhaps your face doesn't wrinkle well. Perhaps, try as you might, you still giggle uncontrollably every time you try to talk like George Bush. Despair not. There is another choice for you: the *John Chancellor*. This is the simplest and most straightforward style to adopt, and it carries with it the advantage that people will trust you no matter how dismal the news you bring them. Its combination of accentless accent and inoffensive demeanor is particularly appropriate to emigrés from midwestern wheat farms and small colleges and to others whose bland speech and unremarkable mannerisms give little clue to their origins. Since the people you meet when you wear your *Chancellor* naturally assume you must come from someplace acceptable—the horn-rimmed glasses look *very* distinguished—you can go anywhere in this guise.

Of course, this style has its drawbacks: it works best for a naturally earnest sort of person who is willing to assume a responsible place in society and the duties that entails. Episcopal bishops, grief counselors, and network anchorpeople are best served by it. Since the highest career goal of a true climber is to get through life without working at all (see Part the Third for suggested acceptable professions), you might find another style more suited to your personality.

Consider, for example, the *Eliza Doolittle*, especially serviceable if you are afflicted with America's most dread disease, HLCA—Horrendous Lower-Class Accent —an affliction for which there is no known cure, although Jerry Lewis is rumored to be working on one.

If you have HLCA, your speech alone is enough to scare the horses. You probably call your favorite after-bath scent *O. D. Terlit*, put *budda* on your bread, and drink *beeah*. The solution is to follow Eliza Doolittle's example and disguise your speech defect.

The sorts of people you want to mingle with have never heard an American lower-class accent—or, if they have, they are trying desperately to conceal the fact. Even their butlers talk like Sir Ralph Richardson. To get on with them—the people, not the butlers—you need not change your HLCA; merely add a few key phrases to your wretched speech.

The secret, which works unfailingly *avec les snobs*, is to insert incongruously superfluous foreign phrases *entre les mots* of your speech. *Voilà*, everyone you speak with will be *facile*, if not fluent, in French. *Un peu de* French will set the right tone to your conversation.

Don't overdo it, however; use more than *un peu*, and people might think you are trying to palm yourself off as a French speaker; that could be embarrassing if the person you are addressing is a native of the land of overpriced wines and street-corner toilets.

You will be far safer if you drop the hint that your roots lie somewhere in the Balkans—or the Baltic; nobody quite knows the difference. Use fancy footwork to avoid being pinned down to anything more specific than that. A vague explanation will serve as paste and cover for the occasional slip. If, in conversation with the Duchesse d'Etoile et Montparnasse, you let slip the phrase *Toity-toid and Toid*, she will chalk it up to the defective English tutor your father, the Archduke, engaged during your minority.

If you really can't abide talking to other people, the *Jackie K.O.* may be the style for you. It is most effective for women, although some men have been known to use it to good effect. Based on a bodacious display of arrogance combined with well-concealed talent (optional), the *Jackie K.O.* succeeds because of its practitioner's ability to intimidate others into quiescent submission. The *Jackie K.O.* plays on the realization that everybody to whom social standing is important—from the *Pretentati* and *Glitterati* right down to your Aunt Tillie in the DAR—is, at bottom, insecure. The fundamental truth of society is that if you are interested in where you stand in the social pecking order, you are worried about where you stand.

The successful *Jackie K.O.* exploits this insecurity by projecting an image of complete self-confidence, terrifying *Glitterati*, *Pretentati*, *Old Money*, and ordinary snobs alike by the sheer power of her composure. With a frozen smile and an equal indifference to everyone she meets, the *Jackie K.O.* cuts a swath through every social gathering—a wide swath, since it must accommodate the thirty or forty photographers, journalists, wombats, and poltroons who accompany her.

The most successful practitioners of the *Jackie K.O.* can cut dead anyone from the Pope to Pelé. When you have perfected the style, you will become the social cynosure of all the land—and all society will live in terror of you.

There *are* other styles to choose from—the *Peter Lawford*, the *Henry Kissinger*, and the *Contessa from Queens* are just a few of them that are roughly self-explanatory. They share with the *Doolittle* one basic trait: the recognition that to get anywhere in the climbing business, you must Never Be Yourself. If you do, you might get into trouble. You could express opinions that are honest instead of popular; you might dress in clothes that are comfortable instead of Calvin Klein; you might publicly admit that Fiorucci is silly.

Besides, if you wanted to be yourself, you wouldn't be climbing to begin with, would you?

The climber's vocabulary

One of the many seemingly minor—but actually crucial—grounds on which you will be judged by the snobs of
America is your language. Your vocabulary, your use
of foreign terminology (see below), and your evident
familiarity with abstruse phrases will tip off many (especially among the *Old Money* and the *Pretentati*—the
Glitterati ain't so literate) that you are one of them.

AMERICAN WORDS

Word	Normal pronunciaiton	Snob pronunciation
banal	BAY-nuhl	buh-NAHL
boring	bore-ing	BO-ah-RIIINNG
dad	dad	father or sir
housewife	housewife	day maid
mom	mom	mother or ma'am
drapes	drapes	curtains
Champagne	sham-PAYN	shampers

FOREIGN WORDS AND PHRASES

Word	Pronunciation	Meaning
pâté de fois gras	pah-TAY duh fwah GRAH	⎫ Note the difference between these two carefully.*
coup de grâce	KOO duh GRAHSS	⎭
fin de siècle	FAN duh see-EK-luh	End of the century—i.e., the nineteenth century, a period esteemed among certain *Pretentati* for its grace and elegance. Pronounce any wanly amusing comment, behavior, or furniture "very *fin de siècle*," and you will be celebrated for your perspicacity.
comme il faut	KUM eel FOE	The way it's done; stylish. Pronounce any moderately amusing comment, behavior, furniture, or hat "very *comme il faut*," and you will be celebrated for your perspicacity.

*I know one climber whose career was ruined when he approached a famous writer at an opening and characterized the film (never *movie*) they had just seen as a "KOO de GRAH." "Illiterate," the writer snarled, and moved away.

Trockenbeeren-auslese	TROK-un-beer-un-AUS-lay-zuh	A type of German sweet wine. Ever since every greasy spoon in America started listing California Sauternes on its menu, wine snobs—who occur among *Pretentati*, *Glitterati*, and *Old Money* with about equal frequency—have preferred this all but unpronounceable German word—not the wine.
andiamo	ahn-DYA-mo	Let's get out of here. An Italian phrase used by *Pretentati* in lieu of "Let's blow this joint."

USEFUL QUOTATIONS

Every climber (outside of Southern California) needs a stock of famous quotations to demonstrate his erudition. They can be dropped almost at will into any conversation—and your auditors, recognizing that the words are more literate than any you could compose, will realize you are quoting poetry and smile knowingly. The fact that they also have no idea what you're talking about will never be mentioned.

"April is the cruellest month"   —T.S. Eliot

From *The Wasteland*. To be uttered likewise. The phrase has no apparent relevance to anything but is adored by *Pretentati*.

Hitler had only one big ****
Göring had two, but they were small
Himmler had something similar
But Doctor Göbbels had no ***** at all.
—Words to the "Colonel Bogie March"

At the end of every Christmas dinner in an *Old Money* club, one or another besotted member will rise, climb up on the mantelpiece, and bellow out this ribald ditty or something even more unprintable at the top of his lungs. If you want to be accepted as one of the crowd—and you do—you must have some equally witless ditty tucked away in your brain which can pass as something you learned at Groton. This will do as well as any.

"Come live with me and be my love"
—Christopher Marlowe

This is the most overquoted line in prep school English classes. Use it for seducing rich people, especially those under eighteen, who will be impressed by your sensitivity.

"Ich weiss nicht was soll es bedeuten dass ich so traurig bin."
—Heinrich Heine

Literally, "I have no idea why I'm so unhappy." To be uttered soulfully.

Lockjaw simplified

You will doubtless notice, if you spend any time mingling with people to the *Old Money* born, that the very rich speak differently from you and me. Although your high school elocution teacher made you believe that no speech could be accomplished without the use of the lips, teeth, and tongue in a rich variety of labial and dental vowels and consonants, you will notice that the very rich are able to speak without opening their teeth or moving their lips. Since you are normally unable to *read* without moving your lips, you will be puzzled, and perhaps a bit nonplussed, by this phenomenon. But fear not, you too can learn how to produce broad *a*'s straight from the esophagus, how to summon a butler with no perceptible movement, and how to communicate with *Old Money* in a language it understands. In fact, you can learn the same way the children of the *Old Money* learn at their governesses' knees.

You don't need to hire a governess to teach you, of course—although *Old Money* lockjaw, like waterskiing or demolition-derby driving, is a skill best learned from an expert. If you do try to do it on your own, you will need the following equipment:

1 20-gallon ice bucket, filled, or an eye-level freezer
20 feet of piano wire
1 tube of Crazy Glue
1 hour-long tape of Katharine Hepburn's voice, culled from her performances in *The African Queen, True Grit,* and *Guess Who's Coming to Dinner*

Begin by placing the ice bucket on a table, pulling up a chair, and dunking your head in the ice for about an hour (you can place your head inside the eye-level freezer if you prefer). You may come up for air from time to time, but try not to do it too often, since this will defeat the purpose of the exercise.

After you have soaked your head for about an hour, you will find that your jaw has become completely immobile. (If your eyes start to bulge, you have gone too far.) When you can no longer move your mouth at all, you are ready to begin practice.

Turn on your Katharine Hepburn tape and repeat a few of her lines: "Daaahling, this is absoloooteleee MIZerable," say, or "Daaahling, this is absoloooteleee BEASTleee," or "Daahling, this is absoloooteleee

HORrible." (Try to avoid lines like "Marshal Cogburn, I believe I've seen a rattlesnake"—they will have limited application in social situations.) You will be surprised by how much like an upper-crust type you actually sound when your jaw is completely immobilized.

You could, of course, continue to freeze your face indefinitely and make your way through society with blue lips. But your lovers would likely find you frigid, and you would be hard put to explain a case of frostbite of the eyelids in Palm Beach in July. You must train yourself to keep your jaw immobilized naturally.

Get out the piano wire. Wrap it tightly about your head and neck, securing your jaw. You will find there is some give in the wire, so that your jaw is slightly more flexible than when it was completely frozen, but this will serve as a challenge to develop a natural immobility. Practice repeatedly. Like housebreaking a cheetah, this is a process that can be brought to fulfillment only through repeated application of training techniques.

It may happen that you are forced into a social situation while you are still in the piano-wire stage, or perhaps you will sense your lockjaw slipping, or simply need some reassurance. In that case, apply a drop of Crazy Glue to a rear molar on each side, then bite down. This will lock your teeth neatly in place for weeks and allow you to practice the most perfect lockjaw. Unfortunately, it will preclude eating; you will be forced to file down your teeth to get your jaws open again. Since this process can be repeated only a few times before your teeth have disappeared, I recommend it only in emergencies.

The climber's morals

If you received a decent, ordinary American education, you were probably taught to structure your life around noble precepts such as the Golden Rule, the Ten Commandments, or some other set of basic guidelines for honesty, uprightness, and honor. Of course, if you went to public school, you've never heard of any of these things, which is just as well. One of the first tasks a climber must confront is to forget all these teachings, in any case. Climbing has a special morality of its own, totally divorced from the everyday garden variety you are used to. After all, those maxims of fair play you learned as a child won't land you a desk job in a widget factory, much less get you where you really want to go.

To succeed in climbing, you must embrace the Climber's Code. Do not confuse it with other, similarly worded, but quite contradictory value systems.

THE CLIMBER'S CODE

I   Do unto others in proportion to what they can do for you.

II   Thou shalt absent thyself before the check arrives.

III   Thou shalt not commit adultery with a person of lower social position.

IV   Honor thy mother-in-law and thy father-in-law in proportion to their wealth.

V   Thou shalt dress for dinner.

VI   Thou shalt not forgive—nor forget.

VII   Thou shalt promise everything, but leave a fictitious phone number.

VIII   Thou shalt not ride thy polo ponies to a lather.

IX   Honor thy banker.

X   Thou shalt deny everything.

The climber's conscience

Things a successful climber would be ashamed to do to get ahead:

Your climbing team

If, like most apprentice climbers, you spent your child-hood in darkest Middle America, you probably think that you already know what you need to make a mark on society: good orthodonture, a Corvette, a Dispozall, an Advent VideoBeam, and a Sears, Roebuck Gold Card.

Dream on.

It is unfortunately true that there once was a time when you could make it to the top with little more than an Oleg Cassini outfit, a KLH stereo, a decanter of Johnnie Walker Black, and a membership in the Muse-um of Modern Art. That time was known as the sixties, an era of rabid democracy when anybody could be anything. All we have to show for that miserable social experiment are Twiggy, Lynda Bird Johnson, Regis Phil-bin, and Vietnam.

Nowadays, cracking society requires a damn sight more than knowing Tongsun Park's phone number. Strict standards are now applied, and as we have seen, woe betide the apprentice climber who thinks he can show up at the Polo Lounge with a unicorn on his polyester necktie to mark him as a comer.

Today's climber would not think of trying to crack society without a full complement of material goods. Clothing we have treated with; other important commodities include lodging of the sort that a lesser British peer or greater American movie star might deem acceptable; assorted cars and drivers; and a kitchen midden of friends of appropriately grand name and reputation to whom one is attached not by bonds of affection, but by the exciting possibility of mutual exploitation.

The most important possession of all, however, is a family: look to this first, and all else will take care of itself.

Ah, you exclaim, but I am a lowborn fellow, a lout, a serf, a person of no pedigree! Of course—why else would you be reading this book, anyway, instead of playing a few chukkers with the Maharajah of Jaipur? Your first task, then, is to acquire a spouse or spouse-like person.

Like anybody else, the apprentice climber should choose a spouse for the same old emotional reasons that have always guided humans in making lifelong commitments to their mates: lust, greed, revenge, and the realization that a few simple words mumbled be-

fore a parson can assure that you never have to work again.

Your first step is to decide whether you desire a spouse—generally speaking, a person of the opposite gender—or a spouse equivalent, who can be either a person of the opposite gender with a morbid fear of altars or, if need be, a person of the same gender. For any number of reasons, as a would-be climber you will find it most useful to engage an authentic, full-time, permanent, and legal spouse, whose troth will be plighted to you before God, man, woman, and mother-in-law, thus making it legally difficult for him or her to unload you when the passing infatuation is dispelled and your true colors shine through in the cold light of dawn.

Of course, finding a spouse may be difficult for you. Perhaps you've clamped your hooks into a bed-mate of the opposite sex who has no desire for the benefit of clergy. Perhaps you realized early on that you are the sort of young man who likes to dye his hair pink for parties and put on a dazzling taffeta creation, or the sort of young lady who spends simply gobs of time oiling her construction boots and trimming her crew cut. *Hélas*, do what you must, but be sure to memorize Marvin Mitchelson's phone number, and get anything you can in writing.

The first quality to look for in a prospective spouse or spouse equivalent is money—if need be, it can be the only quality; you can follow the instructions in this manual yourself and leave your boorish spouse home munching Cheezits and watching "Bowling for Bedspreads." A rich supply of capital will fuel your journey to success and smooth out the pitfalls along the way; its source need never be explained.

So settle for money alone, if you must. However, it would be more helpful if your would-be spouse were also possessed of an appalling physical beauty. This becomes even more important if you yourself look like a wart on a frog: when you and your attached one appear together in public, most people will consider your remarkable physical ugliness and your spouse's unmistakable beauty and jump to the obvious, if incorrect, conclusion that *you* must be the one with the money.

When choosing a spouse, remember also that social standing never hurts; if you marry correctly, all the rest of your climbing will be done for you. But make sure you choose the right kind of social standing. If your aim in life is to make the Laurel Canyon scene, do not wed Flopsy Cadwallader Snodgrass of the Philadelphia Snodgrassim. Do not marry Linda Ronstadt if your aim in life is tenure on the invitation list at the Beacon Hill *thé dansé*. It goes without saying that you should always attempt to find a spouse whose social standing is greater than your own—but then, if you've read this far, it's likely your janitor has a social standing greater than your own.

You will find it easier to land a spouse fit for you if you shop among a younger crowd. People of an early age, as a rule, have not seen enough of the world to

form adequate judgments of its denizens and likely will not spot you straightaway as a gold-digging cad.

The ideal occupation for the social climber is the position of French master (or mistress) at a preparatory school for the offspring of the obscenely rich. At a certain age—fifteen to eighteen, generally—the children of the hideously well heeled try to hide from the fact that their lives will be devoted to clipping coupons and hiring and firing servants by taking comfort in literature. They find French—a language that does not overtax the brain—to be unspeakably romantic and romantically speakable; usually, they moan orgasmically at the mention of François Villon. If you can make the phrase "Mais où sont les neiges d'antan?" sound halfway meaningful, you'll soon have the little postpubescent monsters eating out of your hand.

The trick now is to pick the little critter you find least aesthetically objectionable and nurture him or her past the age of consent. Then, at Easter break just before the youngster is to ship off to Harvard or Vassar or the California School for est, you make your pilgrimage to the home of his/her parents and announce your intention to be wed. Be sure to carry smelling salts for the inevitable dowager fainting spell.

What happens next depends on the circumstances. If you are lucky, the parents will probably offer you a large financial settlement to go west (or east) and never be heard from again—and if the student happens not to be of the gender opposite yours, the offer will be handsome indeed. Your first temptation will be to accept it: after all, money alone can make you the toast of society in certain underdeveloped countries—like California, for instance.

Resist that urge—especially if your intended *is* of the opposite sex. The benefits you can derive from a well-executed act of matrimony can far outweigh any that money—even money bestowed in wild profusion—can fetch. Your espoused, of course, will introduce you to her (or his) set—exactly the people whose number you have been hoping to crack. Your in-laws will feel obliged to introduce you to polite society of an older and more well-heeled variety; having been properly introduced, you will be instantly accepted. Eager to keep your hands off the family capital, your newfound family will probably even dig up for you one of those highly paid but meaningless business positions normally reserved for the feeble-minded sons of wealthy families. You will be afforded a proper wedding, which will be slavishly recorded in the popular press, thus further enhancing your visibility. As an earnest of good faith, the family will endow you with some bank shares that have long languished untended in the vault. The income from these will afford you the equivalent of a major general's salary for the rest of your life.

In all likelihood, your espoused will discover, midway through Harvard or Vassar or whatever, that you are an unrelievable blemish on the future of his/her escutcheon. Before you have time to gasp, some Costa Rican attorney employed by a guano-producing subsidiary of your in-laws' conglomerate will obtain a quiet annulment from the local Warren Burger, and you will find yourself unmarried—and legally, never married. Fear not: this will result in some additional emolument for your esteemed self.

You now have an income for life. Capitalize on the connections you have made, and, whenever the exchequer pales, repeat the marital process as needed.

A very young climber

You may face one unforeseen problem somewhere along the line: one of your marriages may not fail. An untidy business, this, but nothing to waste too much sleep over. If you play your cards right, this is unlikely to happen, but it might. After three or four years of marriage, you might discover that you are actually fond, or at least tolerant, of your spouse, and that you have no desire whatsoever to dissolve the bonds of matrimony. In this situation, courtesy demands that you do something about producing an offspring, a beneficiary for the next generation of trust funds.

For a man, of course, this is a fairly simple procedure; bringing forth the fruit of somebody else's loins always is. But a female will actually have to do some work in this process, and divorce may suddenly seem a more attractive proposition.

Once the actual production details have been worked out—information on them is available in books other than this—the care and feeding of the heir can be turned over to a lackey engaged for the purpose; you need do no more than assure that (s)he is provided with prep school tuition and the telephone number of a good lawyer for those awkward teenage moments.

There *is* one little matter you must attend to first, though: the question of naming the young thing. Look to your own name first; chances are it is something hideous, and you should have changed it at birth. (If you are female and have adopted your spouse's name, of course, this is no longer a problem.) You can waste endless hours picking an impressive-sounding name for your offspring, only to discover that it sounds like a circus clown's when you combine the chosen name with your family name. To dub a child Tiffany Lipschitz or Conor Cruise Mazola is scant compliment indeed.

Now may be the time to adopt the family name of your spouse—or, if you must, to "discover" that you are in fact an adopted child yourself and return to your "original" name. This will cause some comment, but you can ride it out if you make the change swiftly and don't waste time attempting to justify it. Don't, for God's sake, go after the sort of name that might belong to the dotty second son of the Duke of Cheapside, one of those silly St. John Sinclair Windsor sorts of Hollywood names that make you sound as if you were named after a cathedral. Jones and Smith are perfectly safe, perfectly good names—anonymous enough that no one will doubt you come from good stock, confusing enough that bill collectors will always be put off by your firm insistence that it must have been *another* Jones who levanted on the bar tab.

That settled, you can look to the name of your off-spring. The naming of kids is a delicate matter, and if you are not up on it, consult the wedding pages of *Town and Country* or any good Henry James novel (check your local PBS listings for his latest miniseries) for some appropriate first names. For convenience, there are several rules to remember:

You can never go wrong with the syllables "Brock"

or "Brooke." Well, almost never, although most families reserve the name Brockleigh for children in a chronic vegetative state. Naturally, in the neighborhood where you grew up, a kid named "Brooke" would have gotten his eyes blackened with boring regularity; among the right sort, though, Brooke is a perfectly acceptable name for men or women. It will be transmogrified by schoolmates into either "Bebe" or "Beezer" and assure him/her of instant acceptance. Likewise, "Brock," in all its variations—Brockworth, Brockfield, Brockton, Brockhurst—is always acceptable. In the East, among the *Old Money* or *Pretentati*, you can also name your child after any of the stops on the Boston subway system—Kenmore, Kendall, Woodlawn—except for Park Street Under.

In California, and among the *Glitterati* (the two are almost, but not quite, identical), somewhat different rules apply. *You must name your child either after a great American artist*—Marlon, Francis Ford, Cher, or Barbra—*or after a virtue you yourself do not possess*—Chastity, Patience, Prudence, and Humility come to mind. If all else fails—or if you live in the Napa Valley or north—you are allowed to name your child after an organic fruit or vegetable. Papaya Melon Jones does have a certain ring to it.

Raising your child is easy, really; simply take some of your spouse's money, engage a governess, and go back to whatever it was that used to occupy your time. You will have to accompany the little monster to the

first day of school, of course, but this will give you the opportunity to ingratiate yourself with the rich and powerful parents of the other young snobs. You will also be expected to attend Princeton graduation and either (a) the child's sentencing on drug charges or (b) his or her swearing-in as a United States senator. Which it will be depends on how good a governess you engage.

A child is a glorious thing, a true gift of the gods. If your child has any brains, he or she will gravitate toward the richest kids at school; you can then use them as entrée to their parents, whom you can exploit for their social connections or for your financial gain in some scheme that will leave you rich and rooming with Robert Vesco. If, after proper prodding, the kiddies do not produce useful connections, cut off their allowances.

The proper friends

Next to family, a climber's most important possessions are his friends. Here, one basic rule applies: the people you want to befriend don't want to be your friend, and the people who want to be your friends are not worth befriending. Among the rich, the famous, and the powerful, there are some people who have attained their positions by accident. God never meant for them to be celebrities, and, as soon as He discovered His error, He attempted to cancel it. These fading stars will be eager to associate with an up-and-coming sort like yourself. Shun them. If Spiro Agnew invites you over for checkers, tell him you're busy. Ignore invitations to the Mike Douglas Pro-Am-Invitational. Return love letters from Fanne Foxe marked "Deceased."

The truly rich and famous will not want to befriend you simply because you are neither rich nor famous; *Pretentati, Glitterati,* and *Old Money* snobs enjoy only each other's company. Burt Reynolds plays tennis with John Paul II; Kissinger takes ski trips with Greta Garbo; Hua Kuo Feng plays Mah-Jongg with Shecky Greene. People of this caliber understand each other and the pressures and demands that fame engenders; they find each other's company relaxing. The company of the non-famous—people like yourself, for instance—is unspeakably taxing to them. It is unconscionably tiresome to answer the same old questions over and over again: Do you wear anything under your cassock? Was it hard for you to learn Chinese? How do you like working Vegas?

You may find yourself unable to cultivate a direct friendship with the famous, but indirect friendships are easy to arrange. Find out who the celebrity you wish to know hangs out with, and work from there. Open a Christmas Club account at Bebe Rebozo's bank, or have lunch every day at Jilly's. Buy drinks for Jack Nicklaus's caddy or Tracy Austin's ballboy. You could, of course, eliminate the middleman by becoming a celebrity dentist or a Beverly Hills poodle groomer, but the whole object of climbing is to expend the least possible amount of effort.

After you have spent enough time hanging out with these familiar faces, you will become a familiar face yourself, and as long as you remain unobtrusive, you can enjoy all the benefits of celebrity friendhood. These include the right to bask in reflected glory, the chance to appear (captioned "unnamed friend") in centerfolds of the *New York Daily News,* and the opportunity to drop as many names as you can lift. The process builds on itself, and you will soon be invited to more parties, introduced to more celebrities, and maybe even mentioned by name in Suzy's column. With luck, you may even talk David Rockefeller into letting you have a Master Charge someday.

A pied à terre

To billet your family and entertain your friends, you will, of course, need a home. If you have chosen your spouse properly, this will be no problem; simply move into a spare that the family isn't using. If the family doesn't have any extras—or if you have married into an oil-well dynasty from Psoriasis, Arkansas, and would just as soon live a little closer to civilization—choose carefully. Your home will mark you for life.

Your first job is choosing a neighborhood. There are several good ways of accomplishing this. One is to eavesdrop in a bar frequented by second-story men; where the pickings are highest is where you want to live. You might also look for apartments in New York co-op buildings that have rejected Richard Nixon or Gloria Vanderbilt. In Chicago, call Hugh Hefner and ask him whether the bunny hutch is being split into condominiums. In California, the upscale thing to do

these days is either to kick the junkies out of a tenement in the Mission District and fill it with exposed brick and *Ficus benjamina,* or to buy a beach house in the Malibu Colony from an impoverished victim of Marvin Mitchelson and equip it with solar panels. In either case, be sure the young and lovely Hayden-Fondas come to your housewarming. They complement any decor.

One further note: in California these days, kidney-shaped pools are *de trop;* better a chaste octagonal model, heated of course, with biomass energy provided by the detritus of your *Clivis multrum.* Should you run short of an energy source, throw a party for Jerry Brown supporters, and your home will be full of the raw material for months.

The right stuff

To make your imposture of a swell succeed, you must have a goodly concatenation of paraphernalia—or, in your words, tons of neat stuff—to impress people with. Here is a starter list of practical necessities:

1. A wall full of Mondrians

Whether in New York or in Hollywood, among the *Pretentati* or the *Glitterati,* you'll need art on your walls to prove you have culture (you'll need walls, too, but we can't get you everything). Mondrians are perfect for your purposes, since they are clean, neat, unobtrusive, and easy to care for. You may not like them; neither, most likely, will most of your new friends. But the paintings will mark you forever as a person of taste.

You could buy the Mondrians, of course, but that could get expensive. If you join a few local museums, you can rent the things for next to nothing. Whether or

not you return them depends on your minuscule conscience.

2. A Mercedes

Nothing elaborate, just a little silver-gray number
with understated upholstery for tooling around town
when the chauffeur is off. Any number of rental places
will let you have one for a fee you can easily raise
through devious means until you find a more permanent means of support.

3. A club

Every gentleman and woman belongs to a club.
The Smiling Sons of St. Patrick, Polish War Vets, Hadas-
sah, and the Armenian Chowder Society do not qualify
as clubs. Clubs have names like the Harness and Teth-
er, Golf and Polo, United Backgammon, or Ladies'

Lawn. If you do not belong to one, join one. This is accomplished by (a) bribing a member to nominate you; or (b) blackmailing a member to do so; or (c) buying your way into one that has fallen on hard times.

4. A party

Everybody needs one—even John Anderson. Hold yours at your club, and invite everybody: the mayor, the publisher of the local newspaper, the television anchorpeople, Gore Vidal, Zsa Zsa Gabor, and that crowd. Hold it in January or June—when nobody else holds parties—and don't be surprised when everybody shows up. Anyone will come to a party in the off season, and you will have a lock on social success.

5. A couple in service

You might expect Jeeves and Mrs. Hudson; you'll be lucky if you can get Jiggs and Maggie. Your first temptation will be to grow your children to a sufficient age and deck them out in livery. Resist it. Someday you will need them to produce large incomes. Settle for an exotic butler-housekeeper combination—say, some defrocked Tibetan lamas, or Andalusian refugees. They will come extraordinarily cheap, and if there are any foul-ups, you can simply mutter the usual platitude about getting good help nowadays.

6. A summer place

Here you are in luck. The very rich would sooner part with their poodles than with their summer places;

as a result, there are literally hundreds of incoherent old dodderers around the nation who have been incapable of locomotion for decades but steadfastly refuse to let go of their vacation retreats. Hunt around among the spas of the rich until you find a boarded-up but otherwise perfectly respectable-looking house. Then, simply move in. Don't bother to inform the owners—it would only upset them.

7. Sporting equipment

Strew your house with squash racquets, tennis rackets, lacrosse sticks, polo helmets, croquet mallets, and a few unstuck wickets. Feel no compulsion to use them, just make sure they are tastefully displayed. Hide your handball gloves, boccie balls, tout sheets, and other earnests of your true athletic interests.

8. Tokens of eccentricity

Alice Roosevelt Longworth had a crocheted sampler that read, "If you can't say something good about somebody, come sit by me." This was her most talked-about eccentricity; you need something similar. Paper your bathroom with dollar bills, or stable your horses in the ballroom, for instance. Decorate your foyer with dartboards of your ex-spouses. Any of these will get you talked about—which is just what you want.

The wrong stuff

Almost as important as acquiring the right gewgaws and bagatelles of upper-class existence is purging yourself of the reminders of your previous tawdry life. In museums the process is called "deaccessioning." In politics it is known as "deep-sixing." In your case, we will refer to it as "cleaning up your act." It entails a wholesale discarding of everything that has been nearest and dearest to you up to now. Among the objects you must rid yourself of:

1. *Polyester*

In all its forms, with all its pomps and works, you must remove it from your life. Out go the lime green leisure suits and Nik Nik print shirts. Out go the beige pantsuits with Qiana blouses. Polyester is an insidious force; it may have invaded your soul. If so, you will have to get a tailor from Brooks Brothers to come and sprinkle holy water on your closet. The pain of the exorcism is worth it; without it, your soul may be lost forever.

2. *Your Uncle Herman*

Everybody has one. You have loved him since childhood, but.... He drops in on weekends to watch football and belch at the television screen. He has found a store that sells him T-shirts with the gaping holes already in them. He is the only person you have ever known who drinks Hevi Beer from Miller. He will embarrass you to tears when he lurches into your small dinner party for Anne Ford Uzielli. Change your locks. Change your phone number. Move. Buy Herman a scholarship to a bowling school in Peoria. Do anything, but get rid of him.

3. *Your bubble gum*

Yes, it has been your *vade mecum* all your life, your true friend along life's rocky highway. You popped it nervously when you asked kindly Mr. Whipple for your first French letters, and you blew it aggressively into Mary Jo Lortzimer's pigtails. You chewed it to calm yourself all through your interview for Yale—and you spent four years at Skowhegan State Agricultural School reading animal husbandry. Get rid of it.

4. *Your tattoo*

Yes, I know. It meant a great deal to you, when you were in WAVE boot camp at Grand Rapids, to have "Mother" and "Born to Raise Hell" inscribed on your derrière. But Oscar de la Renta will collapse in hysterical giggles when he sees those things while fitting you for frilly whatnots. Have them sanded off.

5. *Your Tammy Wynette records*

Just try playing them during a soirée in honor of Leonard Bernstein. Owning the things is grounds for expulsion from most respectable co-op buildings. If your spouse objects to getting rid of them, just get a D-I-V-O-R-C-E.

6. *Your pink plastic beach thongs*

Tests at the Southampton Beach Club have demonstrated that they not only cause cancer, they also attract sharks—not to mention greasers.

7. *Your windbreaker*

Once again, a painful parting. You have every right to be proud of the stirring victory you won as a member of the Sleazetown Knights bowling and boccie ball team, but, alas, you must part with this token of that signal triumph. Fear not; play your cards right, and you'll soon have a Cambridge half-blue blazer to replace it.

8. *Your Young Americans for Freedom lapel button (or your "Have a Nice Day" smile button)*

The upper crust prefers a more genteel form of right-wing fanaticism: the Republican party. Don't worry, you'll still be allowed to vote for Reagan.

9. *Your hot pink Cadillac*
Ditch the styrofoam rearview mirror dice, as well.

10. *Your plastic slipcovers*
When the upholstery wears thin, give the furniture to your daughter to take to Vassar with her.

PART THE THIRD
Basic
Climbing Maneuvers

The climber's profession

It is a regrettable fact, but nonetheless true, that you may someday have to make a living for yourself. Your stocks may crash, your spouse abscond, your best-laid plans gang agley—and you will find yourself without a penny in the till and the man from Piper-Heidsieck at the door screaming for payment on that last carload.

You will need something to fall back on besides your ample rump, so you'd better start planning now.

It goes without saying that you need a profession, not a job. Not only will your social standing plummet when it becomes known that you are bagging okra nights at the Safeway: you won't make enough, even with tips, to pay the dry cleaner's bill. It should also be self-evident that the normal genteel pursuits of the upper crust are not for you; working as a museum curator or running the Junior League's used-fur shop are admirable pursuits, but they are never lucrative—and the road to starvation is lined with little watercress-on-white-bread sandwiches with the crusts cut off.

For *Glitterati*, the prospects are fairly rosy. Their status, as well as their income, derives from their careers, and their careers, as a general rule, entail no heavy lifting. Nobody could tell you what Bianca Jagger does for a living—but she seems to make money at it. Anybody could tell you what Andy Warhol makes money at; few could tell you why. And Barbara Walters, of course, makes her money simply by doing what she would otherwise do for free at cocktail parties in Scarsdale.

For *Pretentati* and *Old Money*, though, the prospects are somewhat slimmer, and it is to them that this chapter is principally addressed. Your entrée to the salons of the *hauts-prétentieux* can be severely limited if the rumor gets around that you are engaged in an *infra dig* occupation—white slaving, for instance, or producing Barbra Streisand movies. For this reason you must practice extreme care in your choice of endeavor.

If you have no professional training, little aptitude, and a limited intellect, you should seriously consider a career in the media—which, as you may be aware, is the *Pretentati* word for television. Strangely enough, although it is vacuous, vulgar, and dependent on the inanity of the common mob for its very existence, television is considered an acceptable field of endeavor. The former director of New York's Metropolitan Museum, who is also scion (the *Pretentati* word for "he-who-has-daddy-with-big-bucks) to the Tiffany fortune, can now

be seen on ABC, chasing Wayne Newton around Las Vegas as his latest contribution to culture. If some ordinary *schmuck* did that, he would be dismissed as, well, some ordinary *schmuck*. But *Pretentati* can do that sort of thing without fear of compromising their standing. The reason: television pays big money, and in the best social circles, big money purifies just about everything it touches.

Remember, as you value your standing, that not just *any* job in television will do. A job as Willie the Weather Bunny on the "News at Nine" will get you cashiered quicker than you can say Bill Paley. A good rule of thumb is this: only take a TV job that allows you to wear a Brooks Brothers suit or Bonwit's dress on camera.

Not everyone can get a job on television, of course. If you can't, but still think you might want to work in show biz, consider making religion your career. Most respectable jobs in religion require some minimal formal training, so you must decide early enough in life to devote a few years to a seminary; if you handle things correctly, this will be the only sacrifice you will have to make for your faith in climbing.

Choose your denomination wisely: an outfit that requires you, even *pro forma*, to embrace poverty or celibacy is defeative of your purpose on its face; try, too, to get away with as little obedience as you can. Remember also not to go for the biggest bucks, or you will find yourself every Sunday morning preaching to ten million people in a Southern California parking lot, taking in a healthy wad, but blowing all chance for social salvation. Your best bet is to walk along Fifth Avenue (or whatever the hot street is in your part of the world) and jot down the names of sects with houses of worship thereon. Verily, in one of these you will find a spiritual home.

As a preacher, you will want to follow one of two mutually contradictory paths: either you will afflict the comfortable, or you will succor them. Whether you decide to preach a social gospel, stressing the plight of the poor and the iniquities of the rich, or to offer the balm of Gilead to the fat cats thereof, is immaterial. You will attract a following either way, from the rich with guilty consciences or the rich with no consciences at all. In either case, you will find yourself in possession of what the English used to call "a living"—a posh house, a servant or two, and a moderate income which you can triple or so with judicious acts of simony.

If you choose to offer words of encouragement to the filthy rich, you will be rewarded by eternal invitations to dinner parties, and they will make their light to shine upon you with constant opportunities to frolic among them in the Hamptons—the better to understand their problems, of course. On the other hand, if you choose to preach a social gospel, your shot at fame is much enhanced. The *New York Times* will editorialize your praises whenever you call upon your parishioners to donate their net worth to the fund for displaced refugees from San Martino, and you will probably win a Nobel Peace Prize for opposing military adventurism in Manitoba. Furthermore, a high political profile will guarantee your job for life—your vestry will be scared out of its wits at the prospect of firing you.

The pulpit, of course, may not be for you. You may lack a golden tongue; you may find Scripture unreadable; you may, God forbid, lack faith and not be able to bring yourself to preach what you don't practice. (See "The Climber's Code," page 57, for hints on overcoming such bothersome scruples.) In that case, you might want to consider a career in the law.

Time was when any ninny with good connections could wangle his way into a respectable law school; that time is gone, and you will have to develop a gimmick to get in. This should present little difficulty. Most major law schools require elaborate application forms from their candidates. You will be asked to give a good account of yourself, and your career, and your reasons for applying. Naturally, if you tell the truth, you will stand no chance at all of being accepted.

Fear not. Let us assume that you are a college graduate. (If you aren't, go out and become one. Don't expect me to tell you how—even a miserable wombat like you ought to be able to figure that one out.) Naturally, your transcript is execrable, and your law school aptitude scores are just this side of simian. You could doctor them, of course, but that would be utterly tacky. Instead, you will write an application form essay as follows:

"While I candidly admit that my academic record is somewhat deficient—since, during college, I held a fifty-hour-a-week job to support myself and my six orphaned brothers and sisters, and also devoted much time to quarterbacking the football team and practicing for the Rose Bowl—I nonetheless feel that I can offer Yale Law School some unique qualities and talents. Although my aptitude test scores might have been higher, I think that the fact that I did not learn English until the age of seventeen, when I led my brothers and sisters across the Armenian tundra to freedom after our parents were shot, helps explain this deficiency. It certainly has not hampered my work as special assistant to the secretary of state, nor do I think it would be a hindrance to me at Yale. I earnestly desire to attend law school in order to fight for the rights of the poor and downtrodden everywhere—and because the Chief Justice has promised me a clerkship when I graduate.

When you arrive in New Haven, you will soon become privy to one of the great dirty secrets of elite institutions: it is much harder to flunk out of them than to get into them. Since the Yale admissions committee, speaking *ex cathedra,* cannot err, you will be allowed to flounder for three years, your head above water only half the time, and will be spat out at the other end as a certified barrister. Then, simply find yourself a job in a posh firm, handling the trusts and estates of rich widows, and settle back to a life of money. If you ever run short of cash, by the way, don't embezzle: simply double your fee.

There are other professions under the sun, of course, but doctors need brains and bankers need probity, so you will likely not qualify. And, above all, never, ever forget that marrying money is still by far your best bet.

How to deal with people lesser than yourself

As you progress on your upward course, you will find yourself constantly confronted with the problem of dealing with people of a lower social order than yours—people, in other words, just like you were before you began putting on airs. Dealing with these types will be an embarrassment at first; you will feel twinges of guilt because you were taught as a child never to carry on as if you were better than your fellow creatures. You will be desperate to act like a regular fellow, and you will certainly not want to appear to be like—horror of horrors—that dread American monster, the Snob. The Snob, you remember from your mother's knee—or from story time at the orphanage—is the sort of person who goes about acting superior to other people, thinking that he is better than they are. You'd best face up to it now: if you want to get anywhere as a climber, a Snob is what you're going to be.

Your first rude shock will likely come some balmy summer evening as you stroll along the rialto with some rich young thing you've had your eyes on for months. You will run smack into Zits Maloney, your best friend from shop class at Polymorphous Tech and Accounting High. You, of course, have led this new *inamorata* to believe that you were educated at St. Mark's. Summon up all your piety and wit, swallow hard, and conduct an interview something like this:

Zits Maloney: Stinky! Stinky Wartheimer! How's the old wazoo?

Climber: Beg pardon, sirrah?

Z.M.: Stinky Wartheimer. From Poly Tech and Ac! How the CheezWhiz are you?

C.: What sort of game is this, good fellow?

Z.M.: Stinky, don't you remember your old friend Zits Maloney?

C.: Mayhap you are mistaken, sir.

Z.M.: Awwwh, I get it, Stinky. It's like the time you put the whoopee cushion on Mr. Axelbottom's lab chair and pulled the old innocent act to make him believe that I did it. Beee-yootifool! Hey, Stinkerooni, how long did you have to spend in the House of Detention?

By now, of course, the object of your affection—and greed—is viewing these proceedings with a confusion that borders on revulsion. You will soon be in deeper waters than you are capable of navigating unless you can quickly relieve yourself of the burden of this old and trusted friend. You must act ruthlessly:

98

C.: (brandishing kidskin gloves, as if to slap Zits Maloney across the face): I don't know who you are, you cad, or who has put you up to this reprehensible act, but I shall take satisfaction in blood if you do not at once desist.

Zits Maloney will now fall back in terror. Allow him a minute or so to try to translate that last mouthful into English inside his puny brain, then move closer to him and whisper, so that your beloved cannot hear:

C.: Beat it, scuzzola. If you blow this scam of mine I'll turn your keester into pepperoni.

This will give him the inspiration he needs to vanish.

Much harder to deal with, of course, is the problem of your immediate family, especially if they are possessed of Horrid Lower-Class Accents and afflicted with scrofula—as, doubtless, they are. They will display a talent, like bad pennies or clap, for turning up at the worst possible moment.

You are, for instance, decked out in white tie and tails. (These, by the way, are best obtained by renting them from a formal-wear establishment, giving a false address, and never returning them.) You are entering the Croesus Club for the annual dinner; tonight you will be initiated and confirmed forever as a member of the Establishment. As you cross the elegant marble foyer, you notice an old gray washerwoman, on hands and knees, being chided by the club's scurvy butler for leaving a spot on the gleaming stone. You realize with sinking heart that the old woman with gnarled and peasantlike hands is your very own mother.

"All right, wench, you're fired," the butler says.

"*Oy gevalt,*" your mother sobs. "*Mamma mia. Macushla sian van vocht.* Me rheumatiz is acting up..."

"None of your excuses," the butler thunders. "Out!"

Naturally, you want to run to your mother's side, promise to support her forever, pop the butler in the snout, tell the club what it can do with its snobbish cruelty, and take your aged mater home to your mansion, where you will pamper her for the rest of her life. Don't. Simply walk inside and forget the whole thing. If you can't forget, salve your conscience by throwing a benefit party for a settlement house or joining the club's house committee and raising the wages of washerwomen a dime an hour across the board.

The important thing to remember is *always* to resist the temptation to be pals with those below you in

status. If the gardener at your in-laws' summer place likes to remind you that your father was his bookie, have him dismissed instantly before he blabs. If the maid remembers that you once offered to marry her in ninth grade, marry her off to the gardener and get rid of both of them. You must *never* be a regular fellow with the help. If you do, the day will surely come when you will be out on the terrace swilling Four Roses with the stableboy, the downstairs maid, and the septic-tank superintendent when the chairman of the country club admissions committee comes around, finds you, and puts paid to your career forever.

Don't risk it.

Gate-crashing

If you are a perspicacious sort—and if you are not, perhaps you'd best reconcile yourself to a life of carrying hods after all—you have noticed by now that I am presupposing that you will be able to get yourself admitted to the soirées of the *Pretentati*, *Glitterati*, *Old Money*, and other assorted high-thunderers whom it is your aim to emulate. Bright lad or lass you are. Go to the head of the class. You need to learn about gate-crashing—which, coincidentally, happens to be our next topic of discussion.

The first rule of gate-crashing—and I cannot emphasize it enough—is to pick your spots carefully. Consider the case of the unfortunate Jorge Valencia, who ignored this rule. Señor Valencia belongs to that mar-

velous class the South Americans call *lagartos*—lizards —who, indolent, unemployed, and likely unemployable, nonetheless live lives of splendor simply by attending, uninvited of course, the most spectacular parties their countries have to offer. Señor Valencia, a *lagarto* of unparalleled virtuosity, unfortunately forgot to pick his shots carefully enough and as a result paid dearly. He crashed a reception at the embassy of the Dominican Republic in Bogotá just moments before a pistol-wielding band of angry local radicals decided to take the place over. Señor Valencia traded his truffle butter and pâté for a hostage's handcuffs and blindfold.

In the English-speaking world such mishaps are rare. But would-be climbers who attempt to worm their way into the White House with little more than a disarming smile often find themselves rewarded with a month's free observation at St. Elizabeth's Hospital and those

who try to crash the celebration of Yasir Arafat's birthday at the PLO legation to the UN are liable to be pelted with bricks. Ordinary, garden-variety Beautiful People parties are the easiest—and safest—to attempt.

The *lagarto* is responsible for one useful addition to the general theory of gate-crashing: the all-purpose, all-weather, all-season overcoat. Using this device, a would-be crasher approaches the butler or other janissary, who politely proffers a hand to accept the crasher's (nonexistent) invitation. With a quick flip, the *lagarto* sends the overcoat winging through the air like a toreador's cape, to land squarely on the servant's outstretched arm. More than nine out of ten times, the knave will not dare question the *lagarto*, who walks swiftly by, avoiding eye contact and exuding an air of *hauteur.*

Crashing is a fine art; for infiltrating an ordinary party of the Beautiful People, I have never found any advice better than that of a Washington hostess—alas, I have forgotten her name—who counseled arriving at the scene with an empty glass in hand. If the party

104

is outdoors, you simply sneak around to the backyard with your glass and mingle with the other guests. If indoors, you remove your outer coat, ring the front doorbell, and mumble to the butler some vapid excuse about going out the wrong door or having to check on your car. A well-trained servant will never question a guest so indisposed.

You can crash more than mere parties, of course; with a little talent you can crash entire *cities*. My favorite stratagem for doing this was suggested by my friend John Spooner, in his treatise *Smart People*. Spooner suggests the simple device of wandering into a good private club in your hometown, scarfing up a few sheets of the stationery from a writing desk, absentmindedly asking a waiter to check on which clubs in, say, London, have reciprocal privileges with the club in which you are squatting, and then departing. When you are next in London, you need merely write yourself a letter of introduction on the stolen stationery, present yourself at the appropriate club, and obtain instant entrée to the social elite of the city. In no time you'll have a clutch of party invitations and a good grasp on who's who and what's what in the city you are trying to crack. If you intend to settle there, this device can save months of work in trying to sort out the people you want to know and getting to meet them.

The art of eavesdropping

One of the many fringe benefits of your chosen career as a climber is the relative lack of formal education it requires. While the *Meritocrats* are going to Harvard for medical school and the *Old Money* are going to Harvard for old times' sake, you can learn most of what you need to know through self-instruction and observation.

The major talent you will need early in your climb is eavesdropping, so you'd best get on the case immediately and learn how it is done. Take yourself down to a coffee shop near a university, find yourself a table, and get to work. If you listen to the conversation at the next table, you will hear something like this:

> *Student A*: Marx, to me, seems to immanentize the crisis of postindustrial revolution capitalism.
>
> *Student B*: To understand Marx, you must first apprehend the nature of capitalism through ratiocination.
>
> *A*: Then the dialectic must be intellectualized . . .

Because of their unparalleled supply of conversation in which pretentious complexity competes with fervor, college coffee shops are the ideal places for climbers to practice the two most important skills of the eavesdropper: discretion and precision. You must learn how to overhear an entire conversation without ever looking at the people you are spying on; you must also learn to catch every word. This is crucial to enabling you to identify the sort of person you are listening to—and that is crucial to the success of your climb.

Allow me to explain. For a certain part of your early career—before you establish a regular circle of wealthy friends and acquaintances on whom you can freeload—you are going to have to rely on the kindness of strangers. You will become what is known, at least as they are in lesser British novels, as a lounge lizard, a character who hangs out in posh watering holes in pursuit of personal enrichment.

The process works something like this: You start by depositing yourself in the care of a good hotel—the Beverly Wilshire in Los Angeles, the Ritz Carlton in Chicago, the Dorchester in London, the Sherry Netherland in New York. Order yourself a bottle of whatever Albanian mineral water is the current favorite of the *Pretentati*—remember, you must keep your head clear for this operation. Pretend to read a copy of *Forbes*—make sure you're holding it right side up—and set to work.

C: But, Mother, he's just *gorgeous*.

D: Allison, my dear, that young man is the reason the Triminghams' *au pair* girl had to be sent back to Finland.

C: Mother, I *love* him.

D: He was thrown out of Yale for dynamiting Skull and Bones.

C: Those were *firecrackers*, Mother.

D: The dean didn't think so. He landed in the top branch of an elm tree.

C: Graham didn't know the Skull and Bones Christmas party was going on at the time.

D: A woodpecker practically pecked his nose off.

C: Graham's?

D: No, the dean's. Bill Buckley had to swat him with a copy of *God and Man at Yale*.

C: The dean?

D: No, goddamnit, the woodpecker. Allison, I forbid you to see him anymore.

You might want to make note of this pair for future reference; you may be able to vamp one or both of them at some point. But now is not the moment to inject your shining presence into the affray. Turn your attention to the table a few feet in front of you that is populated by a group of black-clad affluents.

E (*sobbing*): Throckmorton was such a good brother.

F (*slightly in his cups*): He was an utter cad, my dear.

G (*enraged*): Reginald, stop that sort of talk.

E: You're just angry that he left you out of the trust.

F: Nonsense, my dear.

G: Of course you are, Reginald. You're green with envy that Sarah and I will get all of Throckmorton's fabulous fortune and you will get none. Well, let me tell you, Reginald. You abandoned your brother, Throckmorton T. Fairweather, in his hour of need, and now, my dear friend, you're reaping your own whirlwind.

Clearly, this conversation bears some looking into. It contains everything the climber asks from life: money, high living (these people aren't hanging out in Murphy's Saloon, after all), and good breeding (you don't suppose Throckmorton T. Fairweather made his pile in the sewage and hauling business, do you?). In addition, you have here two people who have obviously just come into a large sum of money and may need your help in disposing of it. Offer your assistance:

Climber: Excuse me, did I hear someone mention Throckmorton T. Fairweather?

G: Yes, young man [lady]. What of it?

Climber: Throckmorton is one of my oldest friends. Do you know him?

E: He was our brother.

Climber (*feigning shock*): Was?

F: Yes. The old bugger bought the farm yesterday.

G: Reginald, that is quite enough from you. It hardly behooves a Groton man to speak so vulgarly.

F: Old Throckie was a Groton man, brother Cabot, and he was the randiest SOB I ever met.

G: That's quite enough, Reginald. (*to climber*) Tell me, just how do you know Throckmorton?

Climber (*sobbing*): I just can't believe he's dead! How did it happen?

F: His liver split two for one.

Climber: He was the kindest man I ever knew.

E: Yes, he was, wasn't he?

G: How did you know him?

Climber: Just what we always thought a Groton man should be.

E: Yes, he was, wasn't he?

F: A turd.

G: Reginald, be quiet. (*to climber*) How did you know Throckmorton?

Climber (*sobbing again*): When is the funeral?

E: In two hours. Will you join us?

Climber: Of course, if it's all right.

G: How do you know him?

At this point it becomes clear that brother Cabot is

determined to run you to ground sooner or later on the nasty question of just how you knew his deceased sibling. A female scoundrel can handle this problem easily; simply imply that Throckmorton left you with a broken heart and let it go at that. No gentleman will ever inquire further.

If you are a male, on the other hand, your path is a little rockier. Make vague Groton noises. Ask questions of Reginald—ever so eager to rat on his departed brother—to elicit more information about who in hell this Throckmorton character actually was. Don't commit yourself until you're sure you've doped him out.

Don't, if you value your crack at the big bucks, ask *specific* questions, no matter how delicately worded. The reasons should be obvious. Consider this exchange:

> *Climber:* I've been out of the country for the past year. What's old Throckmorton been up to lately?
>
> *G (cooly):* He was in the same iron lung he'd been in since 1945.

No matter how clever a pretext you supply for a question, it can nonetheless backfire. Reginald, of course, would have been only too glad to provide a complete biography of the deceased, if only the climber had waited. Alas.

How to be a Harvard (wo)man

The most successful climbers in America—as well as the most successful *Glitterati, Pretentati, Meritocrats,* and *Old Money*—have one thing in common: they all attended Harvard University, in Cambridge, Massachusetts. In fact, time was when if you did not attend Harvard University in Cambridge, Massachusetts, you could probably forget forever about becoming a success at anything.

But now we can offer you an alternative. By following the simple steps outlined in this chapter, you can become, if not a Harvard graduate, then the next best thing—somebody who looks and acts a hell of a lot like one. It's really not that hard to do; the nation is filled with pseudo-Harvard (wo)men who wouldn't know the Charles River from Charles of the Ritz. But an imperfect impersonation can be dangerous.

To protect you from embarrassing slips, I have prepared the following Cambridge catechism, designed to make your imposture flawless. When quizzed, respond as I direct:

Q: Where did you prep?

A: Exeter.

This is the most often asked question at Harvard. Preppies are the self-appointed cream of Harvard society (remember that cream is the nutritionally vacuous stuff that floats to the top because of its lightweight nature), and to take full advantage of your invented Harvard background, you must create a prep school for yourself as well. Exeter is a safe answer for the poseur because, while it is respectable, it is large enough and sufficiently anonymous—most students never learn the names of their roommates—that you are likely to get away with claiming it as your own. If you tell people you went to Groton, you are far more likely to run into some Endicott Peabody Saltonstall Cabot Lodge type who will fix you with a withering glance and say, "Eh, old chap, I don't remember seeing you at the rugby scrum" and blow your act out of the water.

Q: Where do you come from?

A: New York.

Once again, a safely anonymous answer. Whether you hail from Chelsea, Massachusetts, or French Lick, Indiana, or, for that matter, Brooklyn, you can leave people assuming you come from Park Avenue with this one. Remember, by the way, that Harvard is *not* really a playground for the sons and daughters of the rich; it is a training ground in which the offspring of America's decent, ordinary middle class learn to act like the rich people they will become once they graduate. There are only a few rich kids in every class, put there like bacteria in yogurt to change the flavor of the whole mixture. Most of the people you run into in Cambridge—real Harvard types or fakers like yourself—will claim to come from New York. You will meet them at bars around Cambridge, trying to act as if they were weaned on martinis and Camels; rest assured that most of them come from Chelsea or French Lick. They are climbers, just like you.

Q: What did you study?
A: History and lit.

History and literature is a prestigious but sufficiently dilettantish major for a climber. It is a small but diffuse department—nobody, including the professor who runs it, knows who the students are.

Q: What was your club?
A: The Gas.

Other schools have fraternities; Harvard has clubs, all-male enclaves where undergraduates sit around drinking, eating, playing pool, and mixing with alumni who will guarantee that the young men will never have to go to Snelling and Snelling to find a job on Wall Street after graduation. The Delphic Club, or Gas, founded, legend has it, by J. P. Morgan, is a large but respectable place. Say you belong to it. The membership is big enough that not even the president can prove you don't.

Q: What house were you in?
A: Eliot.

Never, never answer "whore" or "mad," or "the green one with the white picket fence" when asked this question. Eliot House is the sort of clubby place where even the Aga Khan could feel right at home—and, in fact, did. Even in the hyperdemocratic eighties, the house still hangs on to a few shreds of its old *cachet*.

Mind you, this is far from a complete gazetteer of Harvardiana, but it should be enough to get you through almost any confrontation. Most people, of course, will be impressed by any Harvard lore you drop on them—and you might even want to reinforce your scam by sending off to the Harvard Cooperative Society (a college bookstore anyplace else) for one of their armchairs emblazoned with the Harvard seal. If you run into a genuine Cambridge product, dropping a few of these names will reassure him of your *bona fides*; and he will immediately launch into a transport of snobbish nostalgia that requires no more from you than an occasional nod. One caveat: if you live in the Northeast, where most old Crimsons make their homes, you'd best also learn a few of the old school songs for those occasions when some rum-soaked alum insists on lifting his cracked voice in praise of the place.

What to do at your Harvard reunion

Once you have established yourself as a genuine Harvard product, you may want to take full advantage of the opportunities your adopted alma mater has to offer. One of the most conspicuous of these, of course, is the Harvard reunion. Every year, thousands of old Crimsons return to Cambridge for a lavish week of wining, dining, and deliberating in one of the nation's truly great bashes. They bathe in nostalgia and wallow in old friendship, they eat and drink too much, and they generally have a rip-roaring time.

You, of course, don't know any of these people, so you might consider it a waste of time to try to crash "your" reunion. Probably it would be . . . *but*—if you find yourself hard up for cash, there is no better employment agency than a Harvard reunion. Even if they don't remember your name, all your "classmates" will remember your face; after seven Johnnie Walkers, they'll be seeing two of your face anyway. When they hear that you are between positions, they will immediately offer you a vice-presidency at some company or another.

If you decide to attend a reunion, remember a few simple pointers:

Find the twenty-fifth reunion gathering. Remember that the twenty-fifth reunion class is having the best time—and they certainly have the most money. The twenty-fifth reunion class, the thinking goes, has made its mark on the world—and big bucks at the same time. What's more, the bigger the bucks, the more likely that the Old Grad is having intimations of mortality and thinking about how he will be remembered when he shuffles off the mortal coil. Dudley Dufus '55, chairman of the board of Amalgamated Aniline, will feel his eyes mist over when the development officer starts talking about building Dufus Hall on the Old Quad, and he will hardly feel a thing as he takes out his checkbook and writes a number with a lot of zeros after it. Harvard understands this—and so should you.

Remember to look as if you belong. In the interests of crowd control and of keeping younger alumni away from the good action, the college issues everybody distinctive hats, tote bags, and badges indicating which class each person belongs with. Since you do not have the good fortune to belong legitimately to the twenty-fifth reunion class (or any), and if you do not possess the skill to roll a marinated member of the class and relieve him of his regalia, your move should be to walk about

117

in plain clothes. If you look old enough to be a member of the class, and someone rudely asks who you are, simply explain politely that you have lost your badge, tickets, or whatever. If, however, you are still at that stage of life when bartenders ask to see your driver's license, a better course of action is to explain that you are Dudley Dufus IV and you've come to meet your dad, who's already at the party and has your ticket with him. It doesn't matter if the name is real or not; nobody will check.

Remember that these guys can be enormously helpful in your pursuit of affluence. Most colleges, especially Harvard, publish books or brochures about their twenty-fifth reunion classes in which the alums list their current occupations and titles. You could do worse than to check up in advance on members of the class whose reunions you are about to crash, zero in on a few who are likely to be of use to you, and make a point of introducing yourself. Remember, they will be too polite to ask what you're doing at *their* reunion, and they just may take a liking to you.

How to be a weekend guest

You are doubtless aware, from reading your Trollope (or, more likely, from watching "The Pallisers" on television), that much of society's business takes place at elaborate weekend parties on country estates. Whether you aspire to hobnob with studio heads and congressmen or simply ride to the hounds with the hunt set, you'll probably find what you're after at a weekend house party.

In your enhanced condition, you will find yourself invited to many such weekend parties at the homes of the rich and powerful. Typically, the other guests will include the President of the United States, the editor of *Time*, the chairman of Twentieth Century-Fox, the Prime Minister of England, the Pope, and Chuck Barris. You, of course, must learn how to behave with these worthies in order to make the most of your opportunities.

First off, you must bring an appropriate present to the host or hostess. Pawnshops were created for this

very purpose. Visit one—in the scuzziest area of town you can stomach without placing yourself in physical jeopardy. There, in a mildewing pile of junk, you will doubtless find the family silver of some poor sot driven by drink to pawn the last vestiges of simple respectability. At the very least you'll find old hotel silver hocked by a desperate ex-busboy. Drive a bargain for the silver salver, wine·coaster, or filigreed trivet. Dunk the thing in battery acid to disencrust a generation of crud, and present it upon your arrival Friday evening as a token of your abiding goodwill. Since courtesy dictates that your gift not be examined closely, the *Property of the Waldorf-Astoria* markings will likely go unnoticed until well after your departure.

Your first test will come at dinner, which will be

preceded, of course, by cocktails and accompan-
ied by a Champagne, a white Burgundy, a red Bor-
deaux, and a Sauternes. Your temptation, since you
have never seen a selection of wines such as this before and may well never see one again, will be to grab
at everything that's offered you and guzzle it down.
Restrain yourself. If you make a fool of yourself tonight,
you'll be washing down Mrs. Paul's frozen cod cakes
with Raspberry Ripple in some cold-water flat for the
rest of your life. Let the President get plotzed and offer
you an ambassadorship instead.

The next morning all the guests will be invited to
ride to the hounds. Don't. This is not the time to demonstrate the fact that your closest connection to a horse
was watching *The Lone Ranger* at the Saturday mati-
nee. If you try riding, you will end up either impaled on
a hayfork or sprawled ignominiously on your bottom
before a giggling crowd. Stay home.

While you kill time in the house, you will run into a
variety of other guests who, for reasons of age, fragility,
sloth, or incompetence, have excused themselves from
the festivities also. Along with them will be the weekend's host and/or hostess, staying behind to see that
they are taken care of. If you are not physically
repulsive—and if you are, see a plastic surgeon *before*
you accept the invitation—you will find your browsing in
the manse's library interrupted by one of these stay-at-
homes who, having also read Trollope, will attempt to
seduce you. Whether you catch the pass should de-

pend entirely on how useful this person is likely to be to your career. If you want to be in pictures, for example, the retired Methodist bishop of Marrakesh will be fairly useless; the wife of the head of MGM will not.

You will need a few other pointers on etiquette to carry you through. Do not, for one thing, leave the buffet lunch on the lawn to watch "Wide World of Sports"—even if it means missing the Arkansas Pro-Am Ladies' Duckpin Bowl-off. *Do* leave the table with as much silverware on it as was there when you arrived. *Don't* pour your coffee into the saucer to cool it. *Don't* short-sheet the Duchess of Windsor. *Don't* spill your Bloody Mary on the host's white rug. *Do* attempt to make time with the host's marriageable offspring. *Do* fawn slavishly over all guests of any importance whatsoever. And *do* avoid any other obvious climbers who happen to be at the party; associating with them will give you a bad name.

If you follow this advice, you will be a smashing success—and make a name for yourself as the perfect weekend guest. Invitations will come trooping along in gay profusion. This, of course, is good news, but it also presents you with a financial problem even at scuzzoid pawnshops, those little silver gewgaws get to be expensive. Thus, you must learn the technique of sneaking down into the butler's pantry while the rest of the house sleeps, retrieving the whatsit you presented upon your arrival, and secreting it in your suitcase to bring back home and serve another day. Don't worry that its absence will be detected; if your hosts do notice its disappearance, they will most likely be thankful for it. A final caveat: take care to keep a close register of what went where to whom when. It could be pretty unsavory to present a hostess or host with the same pawnshop special twice.

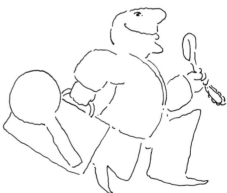

Twenty things bright and beautiful

Once you have arrived, you will still find yourself in need of a climber's most important possession: a façade, which you must keep gleaming at all times. Your façade is not a seamless construct, but the sum of many parts; not all climbers will need all of the parts, or find them useful. What follows is a catalog of the basic building blocks of an all-purpose climber's façade; you will develop others as you go along. These are basic maneuvers and simple strategies, sufficient only to get you started. You will develop the more Machiavellian tricks as you go along.

1. *Society matchbooks*

Whenever you pass a great hotel, restaurant, or private club, duck inside to the front desk and scoop up a handful of matchbooks. Use matches from them with conspicuous display when lighting the cigarettes, cigars, and roaches of your social betters. When the books are empty, carefully remove the small retaining centerpiece that is stapled into them and replace it with a full complement of matches from one of those "1,000 JFK stamps for $1.50" matchbooks you get at newsstands. You should be able to reuse the jackets a half-dozen times or more before they die of cardboard fatigue.

2. *Publicity*

Cut out the photograph from a Dewar's profile and replace it with a recent and (needless to say) flattering photograph of yourself. Take the whole mess to a printer and have it reproduced on glossy magazine stock; leave the result lying around on eye-level bookshelves or desk tops in your home where it will surely be noticed—but not examined closely.

3. *Distinction*

Write away to *Who's Who* for a copy of their latest volume. Chances are that, eager to find out who you are—especially if you write on stationery stolen from the chairman's office of a Fortune 500 company or a major studio—they will send you a biographical form to fill out. Send it back, tailoring your falsified biography to meet your own objectives. A sample for a *Pretentato* with aspirations to power follows:

Climber, Carlton C. b. The Manor House, Greenwich, Conn., July 4, 1940, Alastair Climber and Wilhemina (Roosevelt) Climber. Harvard College, A.B. *summa cum laude* 1961, J.D. 1963. Served to Colonel USA (Intelligence) 1963–70; Distinguished Service Medal, Silver Star, Purple Heart; White House Fellow, 1970–71; Vice-President, ITT, 1971–74; Justice, World Court, 1975–78; President and CEO, Inter-American Petroleum, 1978–present; m. Annette Bouvier 1966. Children: John Fitzgerald, Eleanor Delano, Norton Simon. Clubs: Metropolitan (Washington); Knickerbocker (New York); Bohemian (S.F.); Fort Worth (Fort Worth); White's (London). Author: *Foreign Policy Implications of Multinational Petroleum Planning* (1977); *An Illustrated History of the Connecticut Climbers* (1966); *My Life in the Racquets* (1972). Gold Medal, Squash, Pan-American Games, 1970.

4. *Class*

Scavenge through the used-clothing shops and theatrical costumers of New York and London for a Cambridge letterman's half-blue blazer. Wear it to lunch with everyone who can possibly be of any use to you; if that person is an American, or in the movie business, or a life peer created by a Labour government, you will have to explain the garment's significance to him/her.

5. *Style*

Pillage the society thrift shops for a complete Ralph Lauren outfit. Wear its components to dinner with those you wish to impress. If they are *Old Money*, English, or Harvard-trained *Meritocrats*, you will have to explain to them that you are not a member of a Polo Club.

6. Brains

Jot down the title of the phony book on jurisprudence you credited yourself with in your mendacious *Who's Who* self-description; buy a law book and have a printer whip up a new jacket for it, using your name and title. Cram it into a prominent bookshelf, removal from which would result in an avalanche of similarly jammed volumes. Promise to mail a copy to anyone who asks for it, and lead him/her firmly away.

7. Talent

Hire a student from the Art Students League or CalArts to pull an etching of passable competence and sign your name to it.

8. Connections

Write the President that you will soon be marking your 103rd birthday. He will send back a card enclosed in an envelope with a White House return address. Throw the card away; leave the envelope on the coffee table.

9. Proper Intentions

Go to city hall and look up the boards of directors of the town's lazarets and leprosaria; find one with impressive names and offer to join it. The board will be so happy to find someone who speaks English that they will instantly elect you to membership, providing you with another useful connection.

10. *Family*

A bit trickier, but it can be handled. Adopt one. Don't bother to tell them—poor dears, they will worry about Christmas and birthdays. Simply read up on one of your area's leading, or most powerful families. Then, whenever anyone mentions, say, the Kennedys, simply refer to them as "Uncle Ted" and "Aunt Eunice"—and for God's sake avoid real members of the family.

11. *Old school ties*

Haunt the saloons in the neighborhoods of the more elite schools and colleges—or those attended by the people you want to impress—around reunion time. Drunken old grads will rip off their old school ties and join in rousing choruses of the old school song. While they're singing, steal their ties.

12. *Old family retainers*

When you need to impress some swells, sweep down to the local Skid Row, scoop up a few down-at-the-mouth types, rent them some livery, and plant them at strategic places around the house. Then be sure to serve everything yourself, lest they perpetrate some disaster.

13. *Culture*

Buy a subscription to the local symphony. Ten dollars to the box-office clerk will get you seats adjacent to anyone you want to rub shoulders with.

14. *Good associations*

Open a charge account with the courtesan frequented by the most powerful bank presidents, studio owners, movie stars, and social leaders you know.

15. *Credit*

Using the courtesan as a reference, go around to the bank vice-presidents on her client list. You will have no trouble establishing a credit line larger than the budgets of most cities.

16. *Provenance*

Rip the family tree out of the back of a hardcover copy of *The Forsyte Saga.* Using a light graphite pencil, obscure the post-1900 names to make them unreadable, pour a light coat of glue over the paper to yellow it, have it framed, and hang it in your drawing room. If you want to take a risk, extend the tree from Jolyon down to yourself by inventing a few generations.

17. *Soul*
Depending on the particular circle you are trying to crack, join an Episcopal or Christian Science church, a B'hai temple, an Ethical Culture club, or the Society for Cosmic Rejuvenation. If all else fails, make friends with William Sloane Coffin.

18. *Taste*
Serve Fritos in silver bowls (call them *Friteaux* on your handwritten dinner menus). Always make your onion-soup-and-sour-cream dip fresh.

19. *Wit*
Laugh at the jokes of those greater than you. You will gain a reputation as a raconteur.

20. *Charm*
At cocktail parties, entertain the spouses of those greater than you while they are busy chasing other people's partners. Your social success is assured.

A complete twenty-one-day make-over shape-over plan

If, like many climbers, you have no patience—or intellect—for extended reading, you will appreciate the next chapter, which reduces to basic schematic form the major stratagems used by the most successful climbers. The author accepts no responsibility for the success or failure of users of the short form, and you are strongly urged to study in detail the rest of this manual to learn the nuances and subtleties that make these tactics successful. For climbers with short attention spans, we present: *Twenty-one days to a new—and socially successful—you*

DAY I

PRETENTATI
If you can read, go to your local public library and check out the following: *Vile Bodies*, by Evelyn Waugh;

N.B. For purposes of brevity, we have organized the process around only the *Glitterati* and the *Pretentati*. If your aspirations are toward *Old Money* and you've read this far with no success, it may be hopeless. Give it a try, though, following the *Pretentati* plan.

the collected works of Cleveland Amory (except those that mention animals in the title); all available picture books on Fred Astaire and Ginger Rogers; biographies of the Duke and Duchess of Windsor.

GLITTERATI
Obtain copies of the *Hollywood Reporter*, the collected *oeuvres* of Liz Smith, and the photographs of Richard Avedon and Ron Galella.

DAY II

PRETENTATI
Study the material you obtained on Day I, taking special care not to move your lips when you read.

GLITTERATI
Idem.

DAY III

Practice the following pronunciations, which you will find useful in your new life:
PRETENTATI

Cholmondeley	(CHUM-lee)
Sotheby's	(Suh-thuh-bees)
Cap d'Antibes	(COP dawn-TEEB)
Mt. Desert	(MOUNT duh-ZERT)
school	(GROH-tun)
lunch	(loo-TESS)
Wolfgang Mozart	(VOHLF-gahng MOAT-sart)

The pen of my aunt is on the bureau of my uncle.	(Bridget, fetch my pen.)
Jackie O.	(Jackie O.)

GLITTERATI

Liza	(LYE-zah wid uh ZEE)
Fiorucci	(FEE-uh-ROO-chee)
Rodeo Drive	(roe-DAY-oh DRYV)
Malibu	(CALL-uh-nee)
money	(SWIF-tee luh-ZAR)
Officer, I have no idea where those drugs came from.	(Call Roy Cohn.)
Jackie O.	(Jackie O.)

DAY IV

PRETENTATI

Steal a menu from the local French restaurant and practice ordering. (For a pronunciation guide, watch "Sunrise Semester.") *Important note*: if the phrase *avec Velveeta* appears anywhere on the menu, throw it out and start stealing from a better restaurant.

GLITTERATI

Using any book by Hunter Thompson as your source, memorize the popular names and approximate street prices of the most *comme il faut* drugs of the period. To assure that the drugs are still current, check whether either Paul McCartney or Stan Dragoti has been arrested recently for possessing them.

DAY V

PRETENTATI

Secure your wardrobe; go to the best tailor or couturier you can find in your locality. Charge everything, and take it with you. (*Important note*: If the tailor knows the meaning of the word *polyester*, abandon him.) Order the following:

MEN	*WOMEN*
2 gray suits	2 dresses, imitation Lilly Pulitzer; 2 dresses, ersatz Ann Taylor
1 dark blue suit	
1 pair gray flannel slacks	1 evening gown
1 blue blazer	1 fuzzy pink sweater
	1 pair lime-colored slacks
12 white shirts, 6 button-down	3 pairs shoes
12 neckties: 4 polka-dot, 4 striped; 4 foulard	1 yard fuzzy lime green yarn for the hair (if under twenty-five)
1 dinner suit and tailcoat	assorted necklaces and earrings
1 pair pumps	2 pairs dress shoes
2 pairs dress shoes	

GLITTERATI

MEN	*WOMEN*
2 silk jackets, one with velvet lapels	1 gold lamé jumpsuit

1 white Travolta suit	2 silk jackets, 1 with velvet lapels
3 pairs skin-tight pants, 1 with rhinestones	3 pairs skin-tight pants, 1 with rhinestones
1 pair lizard cowboy boots	1 pair lizard cowboy boots
2 pairs Gucci loafers	2 pairs Fiorucci "screw me" shoes

Important note: These are not complete wardrobes, just traveling outfits, sufficient to get you through the next two weeks until vastly increased sources of funding enable you to put together a proper set of threads.

DAY VI

PRETENTATI

Acquire and study street maps of Hobe Sound, Florida; the island of Manhattan between 60th and 90th streets and First and Fifth avenues; Fisher's, Mt. Desert, Martha's Vineyard, and Block islands; London north of the river (excluding Golder's Green); Paris, Rome, Venice, and Gstaad. Memorize the names of major landmarks for easy dropping.

GLITTERATI

Acquire and study street maps of the island of Manhattan between the Battery and 59th Street and along the West Side from 60th to 90th streets; Palm Springs, California; Palm Beach, Florida; and Atlantic City, New Jersey. Memorize landmarks for easy dropping.

DAY VII

PRETENTATI
Raise money. Get your friendly bank teller to cash as large a check as you can; surreptitiously remove the family silver from the vault and make it liquid; grind up almond pits in your Mixmaster and sell the goop as laetrile. Do anything undetectable, but raise cash.

GLITTERATI
Idem.

DAY VIII

PRETENTATI
Leave town. Leave no forwarding address.

GLITTERATI
Idem.

DAY IX

PRETENTATI
Arrive in New York and engage a suite in the Sherry Netherland Hotel.

GLITTERATI
Arrive in Los Angeles and engage a suite in the Beverly Wilshire Hotel.

DAY X

PRETENTATI
Hire a printer to make up some calling cards giving the

hotel as an address. Establish a line of credit with a limousine service. Open house accounts at Lutece, Le Cygne, the Four Seasons, and La Côte Basque. For references, list the Prince of Wales, the Speaker of the House of Representatives, and J. D. Salinger.

GLITTERATI

Put together a collection of coke spoons for all occasions—those little plastic coffee stirrers work just fine. Buy a pair of red-wheeled roller skates and the week's most popular glitter disco T-shirt. Go home and rest from the exertion.

DAY XI

PRETENTATI

Head for the hotel bar and check out the clientele. Zero in on a likely-looking member of the opposite sex; watch for telltale signs like the American Express diamond card, the ability to talk without moving the lips, the man-servant or lady-in-waiting hovering in the background, the discreetly understated Secret Service detail, or the subtle display of the crown jewels. Seat yourself at an adjacent table and strike up a conversation.

GLITTERATI

Rent a Mercedes, drive out to the boardwalk at Venice, and start skating. (If you don't know how, for God's sake don't start learning now; stand on the sidelines and look graceful.) Keep your eye out for a likely-looking person of the opposite sex; signs to look for include a Gucci bubble-gum holder, Fiorucci skates, a T-shirt imprinted with Lee Marvin's home number, and groupies flitting about in the background. Strike up a conversation.

DAY XII

PRETENTATI
After checking out your new friend with Dun and Bradstreet, send over a dinner invitation wrapped around a bottle of Louis Roederer Crystal Brut.

GLITTERATI
Check *Variety*'s box-office records for the week to see how much your new friend's last starrer grossed. Assuming it was not a turkey, show up at his/her place for dinner.

DAY XIII

PRETENTATI
Dinner in your suite; Strasbourg pâté, gravlax, squab, *mignonettes avec sauce Périgourdine, sorbet, salade, crêpes Suzettes*, Dom Ruinart, Meursault '76, Pomerol '66. Use your devilish charms. Put everything, including the tip, on your bill.

GLITTERATI
Dinner at his/her pad. Bring two bottles of Lanson Brut and a pharmacopoeia of recreational drugs. Your host will provide the alfalfa sprouts, spinach salad, and Tootsie Roll ice cream. Give it your best pitch.

DAY XIV

PRETENTATI
If you don't respect yourself this morning, congratulations. Things are going according to plan.

GLITTERATI
Idem.

DAY XV

PRETENTATI
Move in with your new friend. If possible, leave the hotel without paying the bill; if your conscience won't allow you to do that, feel free to pay up. But remember, the true climber is made of sterner stuff.

GLITTERATI
Idem.

DAY XVI

PRETENTATI
Rise late and lunch at the Palm Court at the Plaza. Then stroll along Fifth Avenue with your newfound friend, taking care to steer him/her to the more expensive stores. With just a hint of embarrassment allow him/her to fill in the gaps in your starter wardrobe; don't forget a stop at Gucci's to pick up the extra luggage you'll need to handle the new gear.

GLITTERATI
After lunch at the Polo Lounge, take a drive along

Rodeo Drive in your new friend's Porsche; remember, of course, to return that Porsche before the CHiPs come after you. Pick up all the little odds and ends you may need, charging them to your friend's account. Be especially polite to any emerald-and-ruby-bedizened Arabs you may encounter along the way; you may want to live with them someday.

DAY XVII

PRETENTATI
Find a party—any party. Your new friend is invited to three or four a night, so go to a couple. Make sure the photographers take pictures of you with John Lindsay, Gloria Steinem, Barbara Walters, and Dan Rather.

GLITTERATI
Throw a party in your new home; make sure Warren Beatty, Bo Derek, Marlon Brando, and Farrah show up— and that *WWD* gets a picture of all of you in a hot tub.

DAY XVIII

PRETENTATI
With a large calendar in hand, station yourself next to the telephone. Receive all the invitations that pour in— probably fifty or sixty—with grace, but noncommittally. Later, you can sift through them all.

GLITTERATI
Idem.

DAY XIX

PRETENTATI

Your new friend will likely propose marriage around now. Before deciding on your answer, check whether (s)he is already married—or, if divorced, whether his/her alimony is oppressive. Then decide on your answer as you will.

GLITTERATI

Your new friend will probably propose a permanent live-in arrangement. Consult an attorney and financial adviser.

DAY XX

PRETENTATI

Whether or not you have chosen to marry, spend the day back at the hotel bar (the Plaza Bar if you chose to stiff the Sherry Netherland on the bill) making the acquaintance of new friends. You can't have enough security in this cruel world.

GLITTERATI

While your lawyers are busy putting together a contract for your permanent live-in arrangement, return to the Venice boardwalk and collect some new phone numbers. It never hurts to keep a few in reserve.

DAY XXI

PRETENTATI

You have arrived. For today's calendar, choose among

the following activities: (a) a wedding, attended by 700 of your closest friends; (b) a fundraiser at Xenon for the Harlem Backgammon Club; (c) the Lee Radziwill dinner dance for the Little Sisters of the Poor; (d) Truman Capote's coming-out party; or (e) Dina Merrill's mixer at the East 116th Street Settlement House. Don't worry about missing any of these; they will recur constantly throughout your life and, like the New York subways, arrive when you least expect them.

GLITTERATI

As a new client, you will be invited to Marvin Mitchelson's house for dinner. Afterwards, go for a swim in Rod Stewart's pool—it doesn't matter whether you're invited; Rod is an easy sort. If your new live-in gets angry when you return home after dawn, gently whisper the word *palimony* in his or her ear. Then get some sleep; the rest of your life will be just like today.